A Short Walk on the Campus

A Short Walk on the Campus

Jonathan Aitken & Michael Beloff

Atheneum NEW YORK 1966

For Mums and Lovers

Contents

Introduction

ALL THE concern at the start was with what America would think of Oxford rather than what Oxford would think of America. Since the late nineteenth century the Oxford Union has sent debating teams to tour the USA. Of recent years the practice has been that Oxford and Cambridge send teams in alternate autumns. The Oxford team tours east of the Mississippi, the Cambridge team west of it. The result of this procedure is that on Boat Race day the natives of Boston sport dark blue favours, the natives of San Francisco sport light blue ones, and the natives of Chicago cheer passionately for a dead heat.

The selection process is complicated by the fact that both the International Institute of Education, who sponsor the tour, and the Oxford Union demand total control over the choice of candidates. When the original invitation was sent by the IIE a small leftist lobby in the Union (whose ideal candidate would have been a Viet Cong mute) managed to extract out of such innocent-sounding questions as "Do you belong to any International Organisations?" and "What was your place of birth?" evidence of political, religious and racial bias, and almost succeeded in sabotaging the whole enterprise. More sinister perhaps was the demand for a photograph, which, if it had been used as the sole criterion, would have eliminated Michael, to whose physiognomy, alas, no camera yet invented has ever been able to do more than justice. In the end our chief rival was eliminated on grounds of potential insobriety (though of course it was pointed out that he always knew when he'd had enough to drink—he fell flat on his face). When the furore at Oxford had died down, a final veto was placed in the hands of the English Speaking Union, who subjected potential candidates to a gruelling interview ranging in subject matter from questions on Her Majesty's Government's policy in the Yemen to discreet inquiries as to how it was proposed to deal with lost toothbrushes or drunken John Birchites at faculty cocktail parties. Here Jonathan's eloquent plea for British recognition of Red China all but destroyed his prefabricated reputation as a political savant. Fortunately, the surviving alternative was best known as a political controversialist for his use of the *a posteriori* argument in front of the American Embassy in London. The selection committee contained among others a representative from the Foreign Office who turned to our friend and said ambiguously "I know all about you already". This apparently clinched the issue. We came, we were seen, and, it appeared, we conquered.

Cherwell, the Oxford University newspaper, had described the manner in which we were selected as "an absolute dogfight" and had spoken of "backstair manoeuvres". Indeed, Jonathan was led to declare in an uncharacteristic moment of personal modesty and party disloyalty, "I was the Lord Home of the Union". The article concluded bitterly "Oxford will be represented by two well-dressed pun-pulling Old Etonians, guaranteed not to let the side down. This means that the USA will be able to continue under the illusion that Oxford is peopled by tea-for-two drinking embryo Noël Cowards who can make polite small-talk over coke and hamburgers in the science and faculty milk bar."

We think the Americans would have been surprised to hear what Oxford thought of her ambassadors. That both came from Eton did not worry them overmuch. Half the Americans thought that Eton was the only school in England and that it was therefore not only right and proper, but somehow inevitable. The other half thought that Eton was an Oxford college (thereby perhaps subscribing to Eton's view of herself) and would introduce us as Mr A of Eton and Christ Church colleges (transfer fee unknown) or Mr B of Eton and Magdalen—a horribly drawled trisyllable. But far from treating us as Tweedledum and Tweedledee, at almost every stop in the tour our hosts would draw first the one and then the other aside and ask whether we were still on speaking terms, whether we fought at night, how we could tolerate each other, and questions of similar nature. Apparently so dissimilar were our views, so mutually derisive our speeches, that our American friends, unversed in the old world tradition that the fiercest of political enemies could be the best of personal friends, could only suspect the worst. This is just to say in a roundabout fashion that the pair of spectacles through which we look at America has one blue lens and one red. Neither, alas, is rose coloured.

There is a need to justify the writing of any book, if it is not one to which most authors succumb. It would be pretentious for us on the strength of a twelve-week tour in

11

the autumn and winter of 1964 to attempt anything in the way of a serious analysis of American society, politics or education. That is a matter for experts, men who practise or men who study what they write about. But for the reader a snap anecdote may reveal as much as the deepest analysis. Travel books will always be written because their novelty lies not in what was actually seen, but in the impression that the sights made upon the travellers. Perhaps with untutored eyes we may have caught glimpses of many things that we can describe and discuss that the pundit might not have thought worth, from his own point of view, a second glance. In a whirlwind tour of this kind lots of funny, moving and exciting things happened to us. Maybe just as a good story it's worth the telling. But together with our multitude of fleeting impressions we acquired a view in depth. Vast daily leaps from state to state might not seem the best way to probe beneath the skin of America. Yet when, everywhere you go, people treat you as newcomers and ask you questions innocent of the fact that this is the hundredth time that you've been asked them, you can filter away the personal and the peripheral, and discover just what it is that Americans think about or want to know about Britain, just what it is they think of, and think themselves. Patterns do, and did, emerge. Above all, for two widely travelled young men this proved the most stirring experience of a lifetime.

We are grateful to the International Institute of Education, who arranged, and to the Oxford Union who sent us on this tour. We are grateful to our hosts everywhere in America, and especially to Dick and Margie Ettlinger of Highland Park, Chicago, for a memorable Thanksgiving weekend. We owe much to the encouragement of the various members of our families without whose help this book could never have been written. And we are indebted to Mrs J. Peghini and, above all, to the tireless Mrs E. Hicks, without whose help this book could never have been typed.

There is always a difficulty in writing a book with two authors and Michael would like to take this opportunity of thanking Jonathan for helping with the punctuation.

1

The American Way of Speech

THE AMERICANS bring to their debating that style of high moral seriousness that characterises their every activity. Speechifying is not for them the pastime of the leisure moment. It plays a central part in the academic curriculum. Every campus has its quota of speech professors or directors of forensics. Their services are highly sought after. Several times we discovered men (or, more rarely, women) who had moved from college to college, seduced by the mating call of the greenback. Of such persons the students would speak in the reverent terms normally reserved in England for the managers of successful football clubs. The comparison is not far-fetched. If one calls debating in America a sport at all, it is certainly a professional sport.

This is not to say that the idea of teaching speech is not one that the English could profitably borrow. It was somewhat shaming to be asked our opinions of the comparative merits as Parliamentary orators of, say, John Wilkes and George Brown, and to be so ignorant of this important part of our national heritage. Students doing their thesis on "Disraeli and His Use of the Dramatic Pause" and suchlike abounded. Classes on "Argument", "Analysis",

15

"A Short History of the Rhetorical Question"—these were the diet of our opponents. How often did we face up to people who only the night before, in response to the dictate of their teachers, had rewritten the Sermon on the Mount in their own words, or constructed a model of the all purpose after-dinner speech! And yet despite its lunatic fringe the basic idea has a core of usefulness. A measurable proportion of both English and American literature is the record of the spoken word. It is as worthy of study as that which was originally written to be read. Undergraduates, reading the Honours School of English literature, who spent their time anatomising old Norse syntax, would be more profitably employed in an examination of the Gladstonian style. The ability to argue clearly on one's feet is likely to be as essential to anyone as the ability to argue on paper, and in some professions, those of teacher, lawyer, politician, churchman, television pundit or teenage satirist, possibly more. Both the techniques of delivery and of the presentation of content come within the scope of a course in speech. This is no place to describe or prescribe the nature of such a syllabus; we wish only to say that in our opinion of all the subjects that we found taught in America, but ignored in England, the study of the spoken word in all its aspects seems to us to be the one that most demands imitation.

What then is the end product of this intensive training? The American style is that of the courtroom; the British oscillates between that of the hustings and the music-hall. At an even cruder level of generalisation the Americans sacrifice style to content, the British content to style. Faced with time trouble and given the choice between throwing a point or a joke overboard, the British debater would always sacrifice the point. The Americans would never have this dilemma since they never have any jokes to throw overboard in the first place. The American college debater debates only one subject a year; and this subject he may debate as many as one hundred and twenty times, on either side. The national topic of 1964 was "That the Federal Government Should Institute a Public Works Program to Cope with the Problem of the Unemployed". As a topic it has all the immediate charm and appeal that stamped its predecessors. For an Oxford debater who is used to debating such motions as "That This Union Should Be Consummated" or "That This House Would Not Fight for Queen and Country" the whole notion of American debate is distinctly alien.

When the national topic has been chosen by a panel of speech professors, the debates teams vanish into the libraries for several weeks and emerge primed to the teeth with statistic and quotation, which they card and file away. Part of the essential equipment of the American debater is to be quick on the draw with his information cards. One team we met were enjoying a successful season entirely by virtue of the fact that they would knock over their opponents' table at the psychological moment. An American debater without his card file is like a blind man without a guide dog. It is worth stressing at this point that the information that he garners is for both sides of the argument. An American debater should be able to produce both the irresistible affirmative and the immovable negative. He may be asked to speak on either side of the motion, sometimes in the course of one day on both. This means that he must eschew any emotional attachment to either case. The staunch Republican must be passionate on the

17

virtues of the welfare State. The liberal Democrat must extol the virtues of States rights. This—and the very idea would be anathema to the embryo demagogues of the Oxford Union—naturally encourages a detached attitude towards political and social issues. Not, of course, that given the topics they chose, it would be possible to work up even a light sweat on either side.

The venue of American debates is the weekly tournament. One reward for being a good debater (as it is the reward for being a proficient sportsman of any kind) is that you travel all over the country. Debates coaches think nothing of taking their bi-sexual teams on three thousand mile car rides to participate in these gatherings. This provides a certain problem of chaperoning that doesn't worry the coach of the usual sports team. And at this point we would like to salute Miss Karen Halversen, the debates coach from Illinois State University, who at a subsidiary tournament of debates coaches at Chicago took the whole of her team of debating Amazons to hear her propose (amid scenes, we were told, of wild enthusiasm) the motion that "Prostitution Should Be Organised by the State". One of the most pleasant memories of our whole tour is the number of beautiful, highly skilled and totally ruthless American women debaters who would so much more have deserved membership of the Oxford Union than the mass of matriarchal mutes who have joined since the victory of three years back.

Twenty or so teams will congregate at the appointed arena (the colleges take it in turn to host these tournaments) and then, allotted to various rooms, will joust round robin style during the whole day. There are no audiences for these debates except the solitary figure of the judge, most often an impartial coach, who tots up the points in the background. During the only tournament that Michael attended (as he knew, it wasn't and, as he discovered, it shouldn't be a spectator sport) the judge remained completely immobile during four rounds, sleeping out at least two of them, and filling in some word game during the other two, while the teams organised themselves in their quaint charade in the front of the classroom. The affirmative team—or, to be more precise, the team who at that stage is taking the affirmative—divide themselves into speaker and timekeeper and, at a moment of their own choosing, they start. Standard American rules means four ten-minute speeches followed by four five-minute rebuttals. There is, as in matters of the franchise, the liquor hours, and the laws against sexual perversion, a certain amount of local variation. Time limits are ruthlessly self-enforced. As in chess there is no going over the limit: the role of the time-keeper is to make sure that his partner is informed minute by minute of the evanescent seconds. The rival team scrupulously maintain a check, ready to appeal against the slightest infringement. The American method is to make as many points per square second as is possible and, of course, audible. This puts southern teams at a disadvantage as their relaxed drawls are innately unsuited to the rat-a-tat-tat pace of the American debate. There is no attempt to inject humour or passion into the speeches. There are three jokes on the American debating circuit. "The first affirmative has used statistics like a drunkard uses a lamp post—for support rather than illumination." "Statistics are like bikinis—what they reveal is important; what they conceal is vital." "The second negative's speech reminded us somewhat of a Texan longhorn, a point here, a point there, and

19

a lot of bull in the middle." This latter is especially popular west of the Appalachians. The other two transcend State boundaries. These are not introduced with the purpose of provoking laughter. There is, as has been said, no audience to provoke to mirth. Rather they are like texts from the Sybilline books—introduced to stimulate the nostalgia and veneration of the judge. It is a kind of courtesy.

The speeches themselves are more like catalogues than anything else. First of all the opening speaker divides up the subject. "I shall prove that there is no problem; secondly, that if there is a problem it is not a problem of the unemployed; thirdly, that if there is a problem of the unemployed a public works program is not the way to cope with it; and fourthly, that should there be a public works program it should not be·promoted by the Federal Government." Line by line the defences are mapped out. The artillery is five per cent original thought, ninety-five per cent research. Every point made must be supported by a quotation or statistic. This doesn't make for enlivening debate—and its chief weakness is that debaters often fail to evaluate the merits of various authorities. Thus the opinions of a Harvard Professor of Statistical Econometrics will be weighed in the balance against those of the Features Editor of *Playboy*. All arguments are given legs to stand on, but some legs are longer than others. Any speaker has, in addition to the exposition of his own views, the duty to repeat those of his partner and to refute those of his predecessor. The debate is really like a game of snakes and ladders. Every step forward is followed by two steps backward: progress is only made to places to which one has advanced before. Since style is unimportant—clarity, speed and a quick hand with the indexes are all that's needed—a debater will not be unduly worried if he has to sit down before he has brought his remarks to an epigrammatic or indeed to any conclusion. Where the Oxford man will end with an appeal to peace, liberty, truth, morality and justice, the American will simply say, "Points four or five will be dealt with by my colleague Mr X". At the end of the day the scores are added up, the trophies—bronze statuettes of Pericles or Thomas Jefferson—are distributed, and the teams go home. After a few weeks of this the teams can debate any topic with their eyes shut, which at least puts them on a par with their judges. The best ones go to the National Tournament at West Point, where the ultimate accolade of American debating is awarded to that couple who know most and care least about the problem (if there is one) of the unemployed (if there are any) and what who should do about it and how if.

For the Oxford debate of course matters were slightly different. For one thing there was an audience. This was something new to our opponents. On the occasion that Michael attended a debate tournament he had by adding his single presence to that of the judge doubled the size of the audience to which the teams were used. It was also a new experience for the audience. Most of them felt that a debate was like a symphony. One didn't clap between movements. It was unnerving to finish up on some high oratorical note and to walk back to one's seat amid total silence from the audience as if one's trousers had fallen off. Laughter was the only spontaneous noise; and since they expected us to show "rye humour" (campus journalist spelling, but maybe a Freudian slip and the American equivalent of our beery joke), that is what we showed. Some audiences had little sheets of instructions passed

21

around. At Madison, Wisconsin, they were told "The Oxford team will be used to people who boo, shout, whistle, groan, sneer, etc." The result was pandemonium, even our tender words of thanks being greeted with catcalls and metaphorical tomatoes. At North Western, Chicago, they were encouraged to exclaim "Jolly good show, I love Ringo, Hear Hear, Yeah Yeah Yeah, That's Grotty." They did, at frequent intervals. The rest was, by and large, silence.

After our pre-debate dinners, we would be left alone for a few minutes, while the debates coach would hustle his charges off for a quick warm up on the rebuttals, massage, gargle and oiling of the file boxes. We would then be led to the scene of the encounter, often a theatre, sometimes a chapel ("I'm going to speak up because I've been told the agnostics here are something terrible"), sometimes a class-room. Usually we would sit on a table at one side of the room with a Union Jack over our heads, our opponents beneath a Stars and Stripes on the other, and the chairman in the centre, at a dais from which we all spoke. The set out was as per any normal TV panel game.

Order papers would be distributed with our names on them. These would be invariably mis-spelt. Atkin, Atkins, Ateken—Belloss, Bellhop, Beelhoof. The paper would inform the audience that the mottled, sagging, unshaven and travel weary duo, sitting with fixed grins on the stage before them, were "Fine young student leaders and athletes" from Oxford University. Eightkin was an "Avid Gardener" (we suspected that the large size of some of the audience was created by those who came thinking he was Ava Gardner) and a Conservative. Blowoff was a one-time editor of Oxford satire (!) magazine (once nature magazine) *Isis* and a Labourer. Versatile Nitkin hoped to be a journa-

22

list, barrister, business man, politician and Prime Minister. Single-minded Ballsov wanted to be Leader of the Opposition. The audience was left to divine who was who from the neanderthal photographs that graced the campus magazines.

Before the debate commenced the speech professor, or alternatively some local "fine young student leader and athlete", would welcome us to the campus. References would be made to Paul Revere ("he said the British were coming, and here they are"), the Boston Tea Party and the Boat Race. We would then be told that we went together like so many fine British institutions, Gilbert and O'Sullivan, Keeler and Profumo (wild cheers), fish and french fried. The tapes would go up and we would be off.

Out of our forty-six debates only twelve were competitive —and for the record we only lost two, both on split decisions. Of course, with the difference in styles judging was very difficult. There would be three judges, all local dignitaries, usually people from whom some donation was hoped for. They would be secreted in the audience in any corner and given little score sheets with such headings as content, humour, delivery, style, logic, general comments. Our personal favourite was at La Salle College, Philadelphia. "Bogoff, faced with an impossible case, took refuge in many wisecracks and quips. 0/10." So really the decisions depended on what kind of debating the judge preferred— and on whether their sense of courtesy to visitors outweighed their local loyalties.

We would invariably start off by abusing each other. By halfway through the tour the jokes were so automatic that we had forgotten exactly what was meant to be funny about them; and black-outs engendered by sheer fatigue

23

would make us slur the punchline, and leave us suspended in mid-pause. The audience, of course, believed that each joke had been specially conceived for their particular enjoyment; many would come up afterwards and say how quick we had been to pick up on one another's sarcasms. This policy was a subtle one because our American opponents would invariably abuse us as well. This gave us the status of underdogs, and won the sympathy of the spectators.

The Americans modified their style in other ways too. Indeed it was constantly averred that they would debate "British style". This meant that the home team would perch a jest on the summit of their usual mass of recondite encyclopaedic information like a glacé cherry garnishing a grapefruit. Actually they maintained a love–hate relationship with British wit all along. They both expected it and expressed surprise when it came. But from what we could see those who previously believed that the British had no sense of humour believed it because previously they had never had the intelligence to understand British jokes.

We learnt other modes of gamemanship. Jonathan's elaborate flattery of the opposite sex, honed in the furnace of the Mayfair deb demi-monde; Michael's puckish habit of falling over any microphone wire he approached within three yards of, so that his progress to the dais had a strong element of unpredictability; those carefully prepared spontaneous rebuttals, that could be fitted to any proposition case the Americans cared to put. But best of all was the spoof quotation. The two motions that saw the Cons–Lab pact were "That Log Cabin to White House is No Longer Possible in America Today" and "That the Power of the American Judiciary is Too Great". The Log Cabin motion was suited to British satire. The American judiciary motion was not. Jonathan's viva-ed third in jurisprudence at Oxford had left him still unable to distinguish between the Law Reports and the Court Circular. Michael didn't even pretend to that. ("My own experience of the Law has been mainly passive... several parking tickets, and an attempted rape charge . . . it failed . . . the rape not the charge.") He conceived moreover the ingenious scheme of inventing a case, each dedicated to a particular girl friend of his. Fortunately, we had but six debates on the topic because otherwise the trick could only have been operated by Jonathan. After giving two genuine examples of Supreme Court reaction at the turn of the century he would fling in with a blaze of synthetic indignation a case which illustrated the judges' thwarting of legislation to restrict factory hours for teenage girls. "Morgan v. the Alabama Artichokes Association . . . Paton v. the Colorado Cottonpickers Clique . . . Lay v. the Utah Ukelele-Players Union." The audience, where they did not sense the festive note of alliteration, would nod their heads appreciatively at this piece of erudition while the American debaters, reared on the scrupulous ethics of the circuit, would go into a frenzy as they commenced the search through their files. They searched for the rest of the debate. New tins of files were produced; detailed checking and cross-checking went on; the feeling of desperation and panic in the enemy quarter reached boiling point. Here Jonathan's anti-file box technique operated to good effect. It consisted in making such patrician asides as "It's no good looking for the answer in there, sir". By the time that it came to the rebuttals our opponents had already lost the day. Not only were they suffering from the psychological blow of not

25

knowing the answer to what they considered a vital point, but they had been so busy leaving no card unturned that they had not listened to three-quarters of Michael's speech. The scheme was never uncovered.

Another piece of local technique that we were able to turn to our own advantage was the cross-examination. This would occasionally take the place of one rebuttal on either side. A debater who had previously appeared in the guise of a prosecuting or defending counsel would become for the time being transformed into the prisoner in the dock. Where our American friends in the role of inquisitor would use the brief minutes at their disposal to probe deeply into their opponents' ignorance, we would use them to score points, though not, alas, debating ones, off our victims. And with women such questions as "Miss Grubowski, may I call you Tuesday?" or "Will you come out for a shake and fries after the debate?" reaped endless blushes from them and success for us.

In addition to the audience and judges, the attendance would often be swollen by various speech classes who would sit in the front rows with pad and pencil taking notes for future analysis of our speeches. Quite what academic stimulus we provided we are not certain, but no doubt in some mid-western seat of learning a doctorate of philosophy is being at this very moment conferred for a piece of scholarship entitled "Wetkin's Love of the Split Infinitive" or "Bitoft and the Non-Homophonous Pun".

We made forty-six speeches in all. Sometimes these were purely exhibition bouts; sometimes they were full-length contests. We never learnt to play to the referee rather than to the gallery, but then to judge by the campus newspaper headlines which informed all and sundry that the British method of debating was to use "wit, ridicule, sarcasm, or personal abuse", our audiences would have been disillusioned if we had. There may be opposition to the televising of Parliament in Great Britain, but a solution to the balance of payments crisis might well be to sell video-tapes of the debates to the CBS or its rivals, for Americans clearly think that the House of Commons is just "one load of laughs".

When the debate was over and the result if there was one announced, the winning team would race over to shake hands with the losers, and we would await the inevitable, the inexorable plaudits. "You were wonderful . . . gee, those REAL British accents."

2

Montreal

OUR TOUR began in Montreal and our visit, following that of the Beatles and the Queen, seemed to us to complete a notable hat-trick for what must be one of the most beautiful cities in the world. Michael took the low road by sea; Jonathan took the high road by air, his political interests having detained him in the mother country where he helped Harold Wilson to become Prime Minister—by speaking on behalf of Sir Alec Douglas-Home.

The boat, the *Carinthia*, was filled with holidaymakers back from Europe, who, treating Michael as a kind of official representative, were loud in both praise and blame of the Old World. When he felt like attending meals (which was before the boat left the Firth of Forth and after it entered the St Lawrence) he enjoyed the company of an emigrant judo professor, a girl student physiotherapist for whom a few requisite muscles were pulled, and a Canadian entrepreneur. The last confessing himself tired of the routine of being waited on hand and foot in hotel and on board, desired nothing more than to resume his rugged self-reliant life back home, a desire which in his case focused on being able to open his own tins of Campbell's Pork'n'-Beans (which, one gathered, was a national delicacy).

Michael's sole achievement in a brief moment of consciousness was to win a Shipboard Quiz on "American Presidents"—a happy omen—but one which only proved that
neither Arthur Schlesinger nor Denis Brogan were passengers on the ship.

An immediate sense of self-importance was created on
arrival at the docks by the presence of several press
photographers—and destroyed when it was discovered that
all belonged to campus newspapers. The Chairman of
Public Events, an impressive sounding if not looking
functionary, was at hand for the purpose of an official
welcome, and took Michael by taxi up to West Mount
where we stayed with Jonathan's cousins. The streets and
architecture gave us an impression of what Britain might
look like in the 1970s. West Mount is the Hampstead of
Montreal. But the streets are far wider and fringed with
trees. Everywhere there is an impression of space, indoors
as well as out. American and Canadian kitchens have the
quality of large size laboratories equipped with a mass of
polished instruments. It makes one slightly surprised that
on the whole the food is so uninspiring. Most traditional
American dishes are European; and where the European
chef will invent a new dish, the transatlantic *restaurateur*
will simply invent a new name for an old one. "A 'Burger
for all the family", read one advertisement, "Dadburger,
Teenburger, Babyburger". There were probably variations
too for unmarried mothers, or juvenile divorcees. Advertisements seemed here to add colour and humour to the
view: whereas in England lights are used for the most part
strictly functionally, in the big cities of the New World
the streets bubble with neon-strip all day long.

Another New World novelty lies in the attitude of the

29

taxi drivers. Gone is the forelock touching, sir calling, and bag carrying servility of the English cabbie. Canadian and American cab drivers treat you as an equal who happens to be getting a lift in the driver's car for which he happens to be expected to pay. There is no partition between driver and passenger, and breezy chit-chat is always expected. "Quo Vadis, bud?" said one as we took our first cab; he then proceeded in the course of a five-minute drive to put a valuation on every department store we passed, and to tell us spicy details about all the hotels. "That's a helluva sleazy joint from the nineteenth floor up but they say those girls sure give value for money." He abused the traffic police as mentally retarded blind men who had arthritis in their signalling arms and did nothing except impede solid citizens like himself, and he dismissed all French Canadian politicians as oily racketeers.

Later that evening, the chief McGill debater came round to extend Canadian hospitality to us. His name was Lionel Chetwynd and he was an imposing figure about six feet tall. The top half of his body was that of a tough robust, international rugger player, but his frame tapered down to slim, elegant legs and ballet dancer's feet. He was accompanied by a swarthy bespectacled henchman who rejoiced in the sobriquet of "Yanqui". Yanqui had a tendency to lurk in the shadows as though he was a sort of bodyguard looking for planted explosives, but he turned out to be the most charming of people. At the end of our visit he solemnly presented us with a little card inscribed "Gerald Blitstein... Business Executive".

These two leaders of McGill Student Society piled us into a huge white Chevrolet and we shot off into the night. Lionel was our first example of what might be styled the

New World Renaissance man. Simultaneously student and teacher, he had as a sideline been running a local TV show for four years. In addition to this he had a kind of razor-sharp wit that marked him out as the twentieth-century Canadian Oscar Wilde. His chief method of telling a joke was to ask himself a question and then give himself an answer, which gave no opportunity for audience repartee. The fact that the next day he repeated to us all his choicest quips and phrases did not in any way diminish our enjoyment of the opening salvo or lessen our apprehension about the forthcoming debate.

It emerged from beneath the cascading *badinage* that both Lionel and Yanqui were extremely ethnic conscious. From their conversation one might surmise that the Jews are more persecuted in Montreal than they were in Galilee under Pontius Pilate. No Jews are allowed a seat on the Stock Exchange, not even Rothschilds; they cannot get into any of the smart clubs, and are discriminated against by both French and English in every sphere. As the French and the English are also at each other's throats, the city is in perpetual three-sided civil war. The only unity is found in the general hostility to the Americans. As far as university life is concerned the Jews have successfully captured most of the major citadels at McGill. All its leading political clubs, its debating society and its newspaper are dominated by Jewish students. In the New World, in fact, Jews are to debating what in the Old World they are to boxing promotion. One might visit a weekend tournament without seeing a gentile from one end of the day to the other. Jewish self-consciousness was marked, as was consciousness of the Jews as a distinct ethnic group by the other students. A passageway beside the old library which provided a meeting

31

point for the Jewish students had been nicknamed "The Gaza Strip". At first we found this differentiation new and amusing. After a while the frequency with which it was mentioned began to turn sour, and we saw that a real bitterness underlay the whole attitude.

In Lionel's apartment (rent $110 dollars a month), situated in a huge modern block of flats, we were introduced to a snub-nosed freckled-faced female child who had the candy sweet appearance of one who had just come from having her pigtails cut off. "Meet my wife," said Lionel. We would have been less surprised if he had said "Meet my daughter". Thus were we brought at the start of our tour face to face with the transatlantic custom of early marriages. Time and again on our travels we were to be introduced after debates to the wives of our incredibly youthful-looking opponents. When it is remembered that graduates are *not* allowed to be members of the debates' squad, the normality of this event becomes all the more surprising. What is more, universities often, as at the University of Illinois, provide special quarters for married students; and where there are none the local facilities, as the Chetwynds' flat showed us, are far more agreeable than their equivalents in Oxford. Gloria Chetwynd, who modelled in her spare time, was the sole provider of the family fortune. In fact Lionel was a kept man. This all added still further to our admiration for this colossus.

During the evening we were bombarded with questions about England: on prices, opportunities for graduates, the quality of politicians and the British election. All the Canadians we met were fascinated by the argument about the abolition of Britain's independent nuclear deterrent. In their eyes, to hand over British control of these weapons would be a disaster for the old country. They thought that this must surely be the crucial issue of the 1964 General Election and were astonished when we told them that the pollsters had revealed the minimal interest taken in it by the electorate. They were much inspired by the Commonwealth ideal though, once again, we felt that anti-Americanism was the motive force. A Commonwealth deterrent would give some independence of the American Leviathan. But they conceded that the fault was not Britain's alone. "If the Commonwealth is really a force, it should be for Australia to send troops to Malaysia not for Britain."

Those who feel that the English are over-critical about their national situation should have listened to the young Canadians whom we met. Lionel Chetwynd, of course, had the phrase for it. "Canada is just a railroad looking for a nation," pausing on this occasion long enough for us to reply "England is just a nation looking for a railroad". But amongst other plaints we remember: "We have no national identity, no national culture. . . . Less than ten per cent of the population watch the Canadian Broadcasting Corporation TV. . . . Practically all poets, writers and artists go to the USA. . . . Arthur Miller's play *Death of a Salesman* is understood and appreciated by all Canadians because their lives are sufficiently identifiable with and similar to Miller's typically American characters . . . this is not surprising since ninety per cent of Canada's population live within 120 miles of the American border. . . . Meanwhile, Canadians spend half their time claiming that they have no links with Britain and half their time claiming they have no links with the United States, while the French malcontents remain only a divisive force."

We argued that Lionel's attitude was just that sort of

33

destructive concept of Canada which created the national malaise, that Canada had a great future and would develop it in proportion to the immigration increase. But according to Lionel, "The only immigrants we get at the moment are those that the American Government turns down." If this moody introspection was a little disturbing, it was at least better than the bland self-confidence that characterised the students south of the border.

At dinner next day we had an insight into the other facet that typifies the young Anglo-Canadian: hostility to the French. Here as in Europe the French cuisine is unmatched, and our hosts naturally took us to a French restaurant. Their behaviour inside was however of such a kind as to make the likelihood of a safe exit seem minimal in our eyes. Besides insulting the staff, mimicking the waiters' accents and baiting the diners, they cracked anti-French jokes in a not very sotto voice. The most succinct and sarcastic of their selection ran "Why did God give the Americans the Negroes and us the French Canadians? Because they had first choice." Unused as we were back home to any form of racialism, it did not strike us till afterwards quite how pernicious the general attitude was. And it was a little odd that they should be so witty at the expense of the colour-conscious Southerners. On the way back home that night we passed Mont Royal, the French University. Our hosts spat in unison.

Lionel Chetwynd's partner exemplified another common type in the New World, the perpetual student. Stan Harrt had received his BA in Honours Economics at McGill in 1959 and studied for his MA at Paris in 1960. He received his BCL at McGill in 1963 and his doctorate of Law at Paris in 1964. One day we suppose he will take a Maths degree so that he can count up the number of his academic distinctions.

Not surprisingly these two were to attack the proposition that "Politics is Far Too Serious a Matter for Intellectuals". Our initiation into transatlantic debate took place in a large hall with an audience of nearly seven hundred, a substantial proportion of whom were the Canadian relations of Jonathan, well scripted for the role that they had to play. We indulged in what was to become our usual practice of castigating each other. "Jonathan Aitken is so aristocratic that his family tree stretches back to the time when his ancestors were swinging in its branches. He is so rich that he has no less than four private dentists—one for each tooth." "Michael Beloff is a self-made man, thereby absolving God of a great responsibility. He got a scholarship to Oxford in History, carried off all the major academic prizes in History, and got a brilliant first class degree in the subject. I should perhaps mention that his father, Professor Beloff, is head of the Oxford History Faculty." This knockabout stuff seemed to delight the audience, who had, presumably, not been in attendance the last time an Oxford team travelled around with these much beloved jests. The only trouble was, as we discovered from remarks made to us at a cocktail party after the debate, that many people thought that everything we said was true. Michael was bombarded by people who wanted his father to get them History scholarships at Oxford, while Jonathan found himself being surreptitiously ogled by students of Dentistry. The subsequent history of this particular quip throws revealing light on the Affluent Society, for never again did it receive anything like the same success. We can only assume that to have four private dentists is accounted

35

normal practice in America. If we had increased the number of dentists, we would have had to increase the number of teeth, and then the mounting mass of molars would have lost any aspect of physical freakishness.

The next day we had to say goodbye to Montreal and to Canada. Here again we experienced another luxury of the New World: a drive-in restaurant where the food was brought out to you. In accordance with a notice, we threw all our greaseproof paper and rubbish out of the car window despite the presence of nearby litter bins—and Gloria indulged in some belated spring-cleaning of the limousine—because this provided employment for an old-age pensioner. New evidence of a planned economy!

At the airport in a moving farewell ceremony Yanqui and Lionel presented us with two books in appreciation of our visit, and Jonathan was warmly congratulated on the fact that he didn't "give a goddam about going around with Jews", though Michael received the ultimate accolade for actually being one himself. Then scampering through the Customs we were shepherded for the first and last time into the first class section of the aeroplane, and lay back to consider whether we were about to find out the truth of Lionel's last words. "The real trouble with America is that it is far too good a country for the Americans."

3

New York

WE FLEW into New York in a spirit of great optimism; but our first glimpse of the promised land was not calculated to prolong it. J. K. Galbraith has written that America is a land of private affluence and public squalor. If this is so, we can only conclude that our hotel was a state-owned enterprise.

Our first feelings of doubt arose when the man at the reception desk, which lurked in the corner of an opulent lobby worthy of the Savoy Plaza, confirmed our reservations. He informed us that our rooms would cost three dollars a night each. ("The Management requires payment in advance for new clients," said a notice.) Since the average price of an hotel room in New York is seventeen dollars we concluded that the management must either be lunatics, philanthropists or Anglophiles. We soon discovered that we were paying for rooms that would have been expensive if they had been given us free of charge.

Our suite turned out to be one poky little garret subtly divided into two sections by a portion of sweating canvas. Behind this canvas stood a latrine whose curious sloping design was reminiscent of the style used in primitive villages on the lower reaches of the Himalayas, and a

37

shower bath which had clearly been treated as a museum piece since the early part of the century. Jonathan, who fancies himself as a pioneer of the technological revolution, succeeded in letting loose a fountain of scalding water to form a lake on the floor, which, such was the humidity of the room, increased rather than contracted during our stay. The roofscape from the windows offered a healthy vista of gas pipes and dead birds. All this had a very good effect on Jonathan who, having previously believed that President Johnson's War on Poverty was merely a political stunt, now became convinced of its urgent necessity.

A little daunted by our first taste of the Affluent Society we ventured out on to the streets—together, as Michael had refused to walk down the hotel corridors unescorted. Nearby was the Women-for-Johnson-and-Humphrey HQ. This looked more like the London Palladium than Transport House or Conservative Central Office. A huge loudspeaker blared out "Hello Lyndon", the campaign song, without end, and vast Big Brother portraits of the two Democratic champions smiled benignly down on the street. Outside a claque of assistants rushed forward attempting to attach favours or stickers on passers-by, and to solicit from them pledges of support. We assured them that had we been literate American citizens of requisite age and residential qualifications we would have voted for their ticket, and were warmly congratulated on our savoir-faire, and given countless badges to pin on our lapels. The razzamatazz and colour were very different from the staid gentlemanliness of a British campaign centre.

After a spot of shop-window gazing (although it was now about ten o'clock most places were still open) we declined to buy such delightful trinkets as a long-playing

38

record of Fanny Hill or a sweat-shirt proclaiming "I love Dr Kildare", and beat a cautious retreat back to our cells.

The next day was spent in brushing up our diplomatic technique. The doyenne of the IIE warned us not to be seduced by the high standards of comfort and luxury of New York, and told us to avoid that appearance of casual arrogance that is apparently the hallmark of the Oxbridge traveller in the Midwest. The head of the British Information Service gave us a little talk on how to refurbish the British image. We were urged to lay stress on those aspects of courage and inventiveness that had led to our island's eminence, and to speak eloquently of a hypothetical have-your-cake-and-eat-it British scheme for a grand Western alliance consisting of Common Market, Commonwealth and the Americas. If difficult questions were asked we could send for couriers who would be dispatched with vital information about the National Pension Scheme or Manchester United. Finally, if a Labour Government were to be elected, we were above all to emphasise the continuity of the democratic process, and to make it clear that Britain had no immediate plans for joining the Warsaw Pact. All this was later to prove most valuable advice.

We were rescued from these briefing sessions by the arrival of the President of the Columbia University Debating Society with whom we were to clash the next night. He was accompanied by a stubby, beatnikish girl friend who claimed to be an art student from Sarah Lawrence College, and informed us with no apparent sense of paradox "It's a progressive college based on Oxford teaching." They took us out by subway to a distant part of Manhattan to attend the Harvard-Columbia football match, which is the American equivalent of the Eton–Harrow encounter at

Lords. The atmosphere of the Fortnum's hamper and Champagne magnum was, however, far distant. In sloping windswept fields oaken luncheon tables were set out, each bearing a little flag indicating matriculation year stretching as far back as 1897 and projecting futuristically into the later years of the current decade. Cole-slaw and frankfurters were the order of the day; and the air was split with the sound of old friendships being reborn, after the cautious reconnaissance, by which each portly luncher identified in his adjacent companion the long-lost figure of "Old Butch" or "Abe, baby".

It is apparently a point of honour for as many alumni as possible to turn up on this occasion, which for some reason is known as "Homecoming Day"—rather a misnomer since the average alumnus consumed so much liquor, both before and after the football game, that he had the greatest difficulty in coming home.

Our recollections of the game itself were admittedly distorted by the fact that during the lunch-hour a particularly murderous gale had blown up. Jonathan, who had got up early that morning, claimed to have seen on a skyscraper a neon sign informing the population of New York that the temperature of the day was going to be 75°. In fact this had obviously been informing the population of New York that the time was 7.50. As a result he had come out in a tropical suit and even an artificial padding made out of pages of the *New York Herald Tribune* seemed unlikely to preserve him for another half-hour. Our hosts generously surrendered their tickets with us, and we left for the warmer climes of their apartment. After a brief half hour in which we fortified ourselves from the well-stocked refrigerator, we ventured out once more, clad in native costume, to hear a campaign speech from aspiring New York senator, Bobby Kennedy.

The senatorial contest in New York between incumbent Keating and Kennedy was attracting far more attention than the one-horse race for the White House. But for outsiders it was once more an interesting insight into election technique. The charge that the Kennedy men had to rebut was that their candidate was a carpet-bagger. Americans don't seem to mind graft in their elections; but they do insist that local men should do the grafting. This was one of many instances in which we discovered that "provincialism" and local sentiment are still a powerful force in contemporary America. To an Englishman who is used to seeing an MP (especially a defeated Cabinet Minister) change a Lincolnshire seat for a Cornish one with hardly a murmur of discontent, it seemed absurd that so much fuss could be made about a candidate who, although living for twenty years in New York, had actually been born in the state of Massachusetts. Still this was an accusation to be rebutted, and the young smooth-haired clean-shaven cheer leader who sought to hold the fort until the candidate arrived concentrated his efforts on converting us to his way of thinking.

"Bob Kennedy will be here in just a few seconds." (A wildly inaccurate prediction.) "You can all see from his record how great he is. You all know of his fine years of service in President Kennedy's Administration as Attorney General. You all know he's a real fighter. Some folks say he's a carpet-bagger, but I tell you he ain't." Then came an obviously carefully learnt refrain which the young man recited with the air of a priest intoning a sacred psalm. "Bob Kennedy was brought up in New York. Bob Kennedy has been educated in New York. Bob Kennedy has been in New York for twenty-five years. Bob Kennedy's home is in New York. Bob Kennedy's heart is in New York. Bob Kennedy cares about New York and the people of New York."

All this was having little effect on the crowd. Our Columbia guide in an audible running commentary pointed out that Kennedy, although he'd popped in and out of New York for twenty-five years, had rarely spent more than a long weekend in it, that he had been educated at Harvard in Massachusetts, that he had only bought his home in New York three weeks earlier and that he hadn't shown much interest in the people of New York until he decided to run for the Senate. One of the best stories going the rounds was that Kennedy's opening speech of his campaign had begun "Fellow New Yorkites . . .".

Suddenly the platform orator had a flash of inspiration. "Bob Kennedy pays taxes in New York." This set the crowd alight. "No wonder New York's the richest state!" exclaimed someone. The financial pride of the New Yorkers, who are anxious to keep ahead of California in the wealth race, was clearly affected by this revelation. "And Bobby Kennedy will be here any second now," continued the newly popular ad-man laying it on. For the next three-quarters of an hour we prepared ourselves for the first coming. More police arrived so that they now outnumbered the crowd by three or four to one. Barricades were erected, to give space, we were told by our platform orator to the Kennedy girls to dance in.

These Bobbysoxers, twenty vestal virgins in white dresses and blue cardigans, stood in front of the crowd and a loudspeaker boomed out the Bobby Kennedy song.

This heroic chant was slightly vitiated by the banality of
the lyrics which ran more or less as follows:

> Bobbee Kennedee
> He's a great man you see
> He is definitlee
> A great man
> Bobby Kennedee
> Will win a victoree
> Because he is a great man
> On November three
> There'll be some fun Oh gee
> He'll win a victoree
> Because as you can see
> He is a very great man

All good rousing stuff! The tune was repeated many times
and the girls all clapped their hands, kicked up their legs,
revealing acres of snowy lingerie that suggested untold
delights in the Great Society, and urged a bashful crowd to
join in the song. We alone responded to this invitation, but
our English drawls, though they won laughs from the
crowd, did not suggest anything by way of electoral
encouragement to the organisers.

The crowd, now growing somewhat restive, started to
exercise their wit at the expense of the dancing girls, whose
marathon gymnastics were exciting a sensual rather than a
political response.

The, by now, somewhat less smooth and visibly less
young PRO repeated all the slogans he had ever learned
about Bobby Kennedy. In between this repetitious display
various local dignitaries kept arriving on to the wagon and
were brought to the microphone to utter some banality,

such as "Hi, folks, hope you will vote for me on November three." Then we were told: "That was Judge Aaron Goldstein, one of the fairest and most upright lawyers in this city. He is not at all soft on crime."

Finally, amid shrieks from the Kennedy girls, the cavalcade appeared. More policemen, cars with flashing red lights, lorries with precarious TV cameras on their roofs, cars carrying pressmen and press photographers, and finally, lurching unsteadily on the hard top of a sleek saloon, stood the great glamour boy himself. Superbrother had come to the supermarket.

Kennedy had the appearance of some juvenile lead, playing the role of an Old Testament prophet descending from Mount Sinai to give deliverance to the people. After some of the flesh-pressing and tooth-flashing, beloved of all American politicians, he returned to the platform to give utterance. The aforementioned dignitaries were all reintroduced by Bobby as if they were old comrades in arms; but apart from Governor Averall Harriman he clearly didn't know any of them from Richard Nixon, and the effect was as if the Queen suddenly turned around after Cup Final presentations and made short speeches about all the players. But at length this period of congratulatory introductions on nonentities finished and Prince Charming was on his own.

His speech was reminiscent in style and manner of the late President; and the peculiarly personal warmth that all the Kennedy politicians seem to generate came across to add a touch of emotion where previously there had been comedy. He referred movingly to issues which President Kennedy had fought for and assured us that he too would fight for them. He was particularly effective in attacking

44

the record of "the juniah Senahtah from New York", whom he accused of legislative stagnation during his last term of office. Among more frivolous references to the New Frontier spirit and the problems of New York, Kennedy told us how his son, when filling up a form asking for father's occupation, had written "Unemployed". "I appeal to your compassion; here I am an unemployed man expecting his ninth child. Have pity on me. Get me some employment." It all went down very well. He finished with a messianic touch. Speaking of the ideals of the American people, his eyes blazing, he produced a sentence, "Some people see things as they are and ask why. I dream of things that never were and ask why not." Unfortunately he never stayed long enough to attribute it to George Bernard Shaw, and with a last wave, a last song, and a last kick, Prince Charming, fairies, chariot and all vanished into the Manhattan dusk. If we'd had the vote we'd have used it for Kennedy.

The meeting had at any rate provided us with first-hand experience for our topic of the night, "That Log Cabin to White House is No Longer Possible in America Today". A sumptuous feast was enjoyed in the Columbia Faculty Club (New World vernacular for the Senior Common Room). Jonathan provided a slight contretemps by losing himself on the devastatingly intricate subway system and emerging into the centre of Harlem. After he had asked several street-walkers, drug peddlers, mafia members and other indigenes of the district how to get to the rendezvous, it occurred to him that although fifty per cent of American youth go to university, he was meeting what must be the other fifty per cent. Scampering down the nearest exit he took another train and finally arrived as the vintage iced water was doing its last ceremonial rounds. Michael, who had in anticipation of making two or even three speeches been coming through the rye at a prodigious pace, was distinctly upset by his arrival.

The debate was held in a spectacular marbled rotunda which might have graced any of the world's great cathedrals. The solemn atmosphere was quickly dispersed by Michael's first sentences: "I understand General Eisenhower was once in charge here at Columbia. It must be the only university in the world at which the intellectual qualifications needed to become President are less than those needed to become a student." The wife of the Dean later told him that in America etiquette demanded that one only made jokes about General Eisenhower in private. Quite how daring this sally in fact was is shown by the fact that when our hosts in Chicago read the above paragraph in first draft they added a gloss in the margin: "Did he really!!! Wow!" as if Michael had written that he had walked through the White House in the nude.

The Columbia debate took place in a genial atmosphere of cultured tranquillity, even if one of our opponents had a sense of humour about as light as a Sunday edition of the *New York Times*. At the end, by the peculiar lottery of debate judging, we were declared winners. "Charm beats logic" declared the Columbia newspaper, perhaps not without reason.

Next day we debated at Queens College. We were collected from our so-called hotel by a member of the Queens debating team (we had no difficulty in recognising a respectable man in that foyer) and hurtled at spine-chilling velocity out to Flushing, in what our driver apologised for as being an "ancient jalopy" but which by English standards was a newish limousine. The poverty line as applied to New York students did not exclude the possession of a car. Their professors were not usually so lucky—and indeed in most universities we found that it was the student who drove the professor around rather than vice versa.

The Queens campus has less of an atmosphere of traditional antiquity and glamour than Columbia. We were led through endless tunnels inside gleaming chromium and concrete buildings until we reached the office of a young man who was introduced to us as the Professor of Voibal Cahmoonicashuns.

We were handed a copy of the Queens newspaper which bore a banner headline "Today noon! Come Gape at the 2 (Count 'em) 2 Oxford Debaters." The sub-line was entitled "The British are coming! Debaters man your wits." The debate itself took place at midday in the free hour between the last class and the lunch break. For this reason we were constantly interrupted at the start by the scholastic coming in, and at the end by the gourmands going out. The slow transformation from visiting celebrities to side-show performers was, it seemed, beginning.

The student population of Queens University is eighty-five per cent Jewish and, as one expects, this produces an atmosphere of greater intellectual endeavour and less promiscuity.

The Columbia students are by and large boarders, the Queens' ones "dayboys" and "daygirls" who according to their speech professor, once they had returned home to the clutches of the Jewish mommas, were protected from the lures of the big city. The temptation, however, for the jeunes gens of Columbia and their "progressive" young

47

amours to sow their wild oats when many hundreds of miles away from home, and cloaked by the anonymity of the metropolis, is apparently irresistible. It seems that at certain seasons in the year smart hotels in New York offer a five-dollar-a-day rate for students. When this rate is available it is snapped up by enterprising Columbia-ites who regularly shack up, thirty or forty at a time, for their luxurious immoral weekends in these establishments.

Be that as it may, we found that our more continent hosts from Queens were no less amusing than their sophisticated counterparts. And in the great tradition of Jewish wit that has embellished American entertainment from the Marx brothers through Danny Kaye to Phil Silvers and Mort Sahl, we place the sign in their lavatory, "In the event of a nuclear attack, hide beneath this urinal. It's never been hit yet."

During our five days in New York we were enveloped in the social whirl of the beau monde. We swiftly discovered that, unlike in England, it is not actually necessary to know the hosts to be invited to a party; rather one is invited to a party to be got to be known. Evening parties in New York begin after dinner—that is at about five in the afternoon. The unsuspecting foreign guest who has not taken good care to line his belly to withstand the assault of the American cocktail may find himself in a position where, on being asked whether he prefers Bourbons, he thinks that his views are being canvassed on the future of the monarchy in France. That at any rate was Michael's explanation for talking about the Comte de Paris for forty minutes to a waiter.

There were diplomatic parties at which we were able to pick up all the latest arguments for our debate on the

United Nations; and to watch the hostilities of the assembly
floor melt away in the permissive atmosphere of a Manhattan penthouse, so that the only cold war was concerned
with who would have inspection rights over the cheese
dip, and the only veto was on whether or not we could
invade the roof garden. There were journalistic parties
where everybody talked about politics and political parties
at which everybody talked about journalists; "arty"
parties and hearty parties; and parties at which the only
exercise was to drop names for other people's benefit,
where we were known in the deathless phrase of one
sophisticate as the "boys from the college that Mrs
Simpson's husband went to".

One party which Jonathan infiltrated by virtue of being
a friend of a friend of the hostess's and which was peculiarly
fascinating was given in order to rally support among the
financial, social, political and artistic élite for Bobby
Kennedy's campaign for the US Senate. The hostess had
assembled a glamorous caucus of the rich, the famous and
the beautiful, all of which categories the well-scrubbed
Jonathan pretended to enhance.

Jonathan, however, was slow to realise the nature of the
concourse, and was singularly inept at making conversation. For example, he was introduced to Leonard Bernstein, a name revered world wide as the conductor of the
New York Symphony Orchestra. Jonathan vaguely
remembered that he had heard the name somewhere
before and on a random shot spent twenty minutes trying
to discover precisely what Mr Bernstein did in New York's
political hierarchy, a discovery made more difficult by the
fact that when Mr Bernstein spoke of "Mahler's composi-
tions" his transatlantic pronunciation deceived Jonathan

49

into deciding that the subject under discussion was Norman Mailer's novels.

At this point Mrs Jacqueline Kennedy entered—and a brief introduction gave Jonathan the chance the next day to make the one-up remark of a life-time. Explaining why he had cut a date with some local girl to attend the party, he was able to say, "My dear. There is only one woman in the world for whom I would stand you up. . . ."

At length the party became segregated into the high and the mighty—and even the mighty were becoming somewhat high. Therefore without much further ado Arthur Schlessinger, historian and former Presidential aide, gave a witty and entertaining speech to the assembled company. It was one of Mr Schlessinger's shorter addresses, and the audience enjoyed every hour of it. "I am here in the absence of Gore Vidal to make some remarks about Bobby Kennedy," he began. He produced a string of erudite historical precedents which proved that carpet-baggers make good senators; he praised Bobby Kennedy's personal qualities and his contribution to foreign affairs, and made much of the undeniable point that Senator Keating was in no way intellectual.

After the Schlessinger oration a lumbering giant took the floor and revealed himself as the Affluent Society's own J. K. Galbraith. "In your heart you know Arthur's right," he started, and in an excellent short speech he re-emphasised all the virtues of Bobby. The cocktail drinkers had now had their fill of politics and there was a surge of movement in the direction of the drinks table.

The speakers were, however, by no means exhausted and invited questions, which were asked by those who could make their voices heard above the clatter of clinking glasses and non-political gossip that was going on in the background. Miss Lauren Bacall acted as a sort of referee between the noise-making politicians and the noise-making drinkers.

"Silencia," she would shout imperiously every few minutes. Arthur Schlessinger at first thought it referred to him (Schlesingia?) and so the drinkers were allowed to make more noise. However, shouts from this glamorous actress convinced the drinkers that they were the objects of her comments so they briefly subsided into silence and the questioning went on. They did not, though, subside for very long and during the next forty minutes or so there was a distinct feeling of competition between the two groups. After a time the questions deteriorated somewhat both in quality and lucidity.

Mrs Kennedy, who had been observed yawning, slipped discreetly away; Ambassador Galbraith announced simply that he must dash to catch a plane to India. The hubbub from the drinkers grew louder. Someone fell off a chair and knocked over an aspidistra. Shrill laughter drowned the serious political discussion and Arthur Schlessinger gracefully abdicated his position as mentor to the intoxicate.

By this time it had become clear even to greenhorns like ourselves that American high political society was graded according to the games one played. In the days of Ike a man had status if he played a round with "the great white golfer" as a satirical friend of ours called him. With the advent of the New Frontier touch football at Hyannis Port was the "thing". But in the era of the Great Society the sure mark of being on the inside was to have swum alongside LBJ in the White House pool. In the modern hall of fame was placed our host of the next evening, Marvin Kantor, a Vice-President of the Curtis Publishing Company, whose reputed salary of $100,000 p.a. sat easily on his vicuna-coated shoulders. On the night that we dined with him in a superb restaurant on Forty-Second Street, Kantor was in the midst of a battle for control of the company. So after high politics, a glimpse of high finance! Before the meal we were introduced to the cowering attorneys who were at the storm centre, and whom Kantor and his ally treated rather as if they were prize fighters in whom they had invested some speculative income. "You're gonna kill 'em come Monday," he would repeat. "That's the day, my boys. Either they sink or we sink, and we sure ain't giving them no lifebelts." The attorneys spluttered into their tomato juices and assented. Over dinner itself we witnessed in awe how a telephone was attached to the table, and after the hors d'oeuvre the magnate would call up associates in various places over the continent and bark out instructions for the coming fray. By the time that the fish had arrived one telephone was clearly inadequate, and a further one was brought. By the time we had reached the apple pie à la mode the table resembled an office in a hurricane with calls coming in and going out on all sides.

American businessmen, however, do not, as we discovered spend their whole time in creating empires of industry and communications. The next day we attached ourselves to the train of another executive, Henry G. Walter, Junior, who is President of the exotically named International Flavours and Fragrances Incorporated. A hydrofoil had been chartered to take his top executives to the World's Fair by way of the East River. The reactions of these captains of industry to the Fair was somewhat startling. Not for them the pavilions, showrooms filled with the best machinery of the next decade. A bee-line was made for the Pepsi Cola Palace. We were shepherded by two clowns wearing giant sized Droopy and Mickey Mouse masks on to a wooden pier, whence we embarked, after a lot of shoving for the best places by exuberant executives, into little wooden boats which set sail down a narrow stream of water and entered a large cavern. It was, we thought, a tunnel of love.

The similarity ended once we entered the cavern, for bright lights gleamed everywhere revealing thousands of beautifully made and lavishly dressed wooden puppets in perpetual motion. Their jaws opening and shutting with clockwork regularity boomed out in a chorus of five hundred falsetto trebles words which are indelibly stamped on our memory:

> It's a world of laughter, a world of fun
> It's a world that's only just begun
> It's a world of joy for everyone
> It's a small, small small world

It was almost fit to be adapted to a political purpose. We thought from the nature of the entertainment that there must have been some mistake. The International Flavours and Fragrances Corporation had surely intended to attend the scientific pavilion and had by mistake got into the queue for the under fives. Not so. The executives were living it up, pointing enthusiastically at certain puppets, joining in the chorus of the song with a high degree of accuracy and rocking the paddle boats with great gales of laughter and much slapping of thighs.

53

We were next taken to the Johnson Pavilion, where after the showing of a nature film, all the business men rose to their feet and started to sniff in harmony. Our guide proudly informed us that the company had scented the cinema. We too sniffed appreciatively at the air but could discern nothing. One of us was bold enough to say so. The reply was a scornful chuckle at our ignorance of the science of odours. "That's just how it should be," he said. "We eliminated all smells by blending other smells."

Our last port of call was to the Spanish Pavilion where we all stood in front of Goya's Naked Maja and made comments like "Gee, that broad sure had some tits," or "Hey, take a load of that tottsie." After this lightning "doing" of the World's Fair, which ranks with the ten-minute Louvre as a great feat of American sightseeing, we adjourned for lunch.

Our final experience in the social world came with our attendance of the Broadway première (and, alas, dernière) of the show "Hang Down Your Head and Die". This was no ordinary production from our point of view because it had originated in undergraduate Oxford. The University Experimental Theatre Club had been experimenting in a form of theatrical enterprise known as "total theatre", out of which had been born this fabulously successful, half-comic, half-serious show on the theme of abolishing capital punishment.

The invitation to this exclusively off-Broadway occasion specified black ties as the apparel. As we had always believed that the dinner jacket was obsolete in God's own country, we were unequipped for an appearance, and had to take refuge in a near literal construction of the words, sporting a black tie with our very unblack daytime lounge

54

suits. To camouflage ourselves we arrived an hour early for the performance, and skulked at the back of the auditorium in the artificial twilight which concealed the enormity of our affront from passing programme sellers, ice cream vendors and even, half an hour or so after the show began, the invitees.

"Hand Down Your Head", as it was referred to among the cognoscenti, was the theatrical sister of Joan Littlewood's "Oh What a Lovely War". Its structure was of dances, songs, statistics, mime and set pieces that were built into a passionate indictment of legalised execution.

The American producer was Mrs Marion Javits, wife of the senior New York Republican Senator Jacob K. Javits. It was, in fact, Mrs Javits' debut as a producer and on this first night it appeared that she had got her twin roles of Republican politician's wife and patronne of radical theatrical enterprise seriously confused, for she had invited to the first night all her husband's leading wealthy Republican friends.

Republicans, especially in AD 1964, are not noted for their devotion to liberal causes. They could not be expected to look favourably upon propaganda for the abolition of the death penalty. This fact appeared to have escaped Mrs Javits, but she must soon have realised something was wrong.

As the show progressed with such central items as the rock'n'roll number "Give me Gas", and the calypso on Royal Commissions, eyes began to turn rather to the fashion show that the audience were putting on amongst themselves than to the perspiring protagonists of "total theatre". Even a sketch devoted to the electrocution of the Rosenbergs failed to arouse any gleam of patriotic appreciation amongst them. This episode focuses on the incredible length of time that it took the Rosenbergs to die. For that fifty-seven seconds nothing happens upon stage, and a spotlight beams relentlessly on an empty chair. At Oxford this piece had brought tears to people's eyes, but in New York a lot of the audience clearly thought that electrocution was far too good a death for the Rosenbergs, and were wholly unimpressed. When the scene was repeated for the "second shock" there was audible restiveness. Silence on the stage was not the stuff of which successful New York first nights are made.

At one point in the play the audience are asked to join in a song, whose refrain is "Up goes the rope, the jolly hempen rope, I love to see them swinging on the gallows". With true Oxonian loyalty we piped away in solitude, while heads all round craned towards us to pick out these blasphemers.

After the show a banquet was given to celebrate the show's successful opening; and we listened to highbrow conversation amid the mounds of lobster, prawn, turkey, lamb and recondite fruits that graced the restaurant, while Senator Javits made a brave speech about the "dear liberal causes that we all know and love so well" and paid tributes to the actors, directors, writers, stage-hands and incumbent Senator Keating for contributing to the show's launching.

The next day it folded: and taking the hint that Oxford productions were losing status in New York we took the road to Philadelphia.

4

Ivy League Land

IVY LEAGUE is the New World equivalent of Oxbridge. It consists of Columbia, Cornell, Harvard, Dartmouth, Yale, Princeton, Brown and the University of Pennsylvania. The only official relationship of these eight schools is that they have all agreed to play a particularly ineffective variety of football with one another. But in the popular mind, and in their own mind too, they represent the pinnacles of the American educational system. And this superior octopus is a beast both to be admired and to be shot at.

Americans like to call America "God's own country". But though since 1776 they have ceased to be the King's own country, they retain their craving for hierarchy. One of the things that most amused us about the American vernacular was their misuse of the word "aristocracy".

"Frank, Harry and Joe are the aristocracy of this year's football team," said one caption to a campus newspaper photograph of three sinister-looking toughs. The reason for this social promotion was that Frank, Harry and Joe were the only players left over from last year.

"Mr Hickenberg is the great aristocrat of our University benefactors" were the words of introduction to a corpulent

57

local undertaker, whose outsize embalming profits had for years been given to campus building projects.

Of a mid-western debater who produced a corny peroration laced with ham-acted pauses and gestures, we were told by the debates coach, "Jim is an exponent of the ancient aristocratic tradition of American oratory".

We became a little ashamed that we were unable to supply between us even a knighthood, the more so since one of the contestants for a place on the tour had been the son of Scotland's premier Duke. Many students clearly felt they had been cheated out of something. "I suppose you couldn't fly him over just for the weekend," said one heartrendingly beautiful sophomore from Wayne State.

The educational excellence of the Ivy League schools is unchallenged, but what interested us more was their social character. To an American ivy symbolizes genuine old age which *per se* is to be admired. To a British gardener ivy signifies the destruction by slow suffocation of trees and shrubs. There is an element of truth in both these horticultural analogies.

At the University of Pennsylvania we were greeted by a student who, within two minutes of our arrival at the depôt where the Greyhound buses were kennelled, was saying in aggressive reply to our questions about the size of the campus and so on, "It's an Ivy League school, you know". He obviously felt that this label alone placed the University beyond the scope of investigation. He made it quite clear that visitors from England to an Ivy League school could worship if they liked, but ought not to ask too many questions. This student came from Texas (he informed us of this in the same breath as he informed us about his university being in the Ivy League, as though

58

they were equal passports to excellence), and we soon began to wonder whether he wasn't suffering from an effortless inferiority complex. Certainly we never found anywhere else on the tour, as we found in Ivy League land, a kind of desire to involve us as Oxbridge graduates in the local mystique, a wish to prove without dispute that we and they were from the same stable.

There was superficially a devotion to Oxbridge traditions. Jonathan Edwards College, in which we stayed at Yale, with its pseudo quadrangles, greystone buildings and carefully cultivated ivy seemed to us to be almost an architectural parody. (Later on the tour we found a grand-child of the style at Duke University, South Carolina, called by its inmates "the Harvard of the South", where the campus, admittedly magnificent, was built in the fashion of the great Gothic revival of the 1930s.) Yale Hall, which is one of the campus dining rooms, is a very obvious forgery. One tolerates inconvenient serving arrangements, cramped and uncomfortable benches and the heavy lugubrious atmosphere of Christ Church Hall because transcending all these disadvantages one is conscious of a very real sense of Oxonian tradition and history. Yale Hall had all the disadvantages and none of the traditions. As we stood in Yale Hall in ye olde Oxford queue waiting fifteen minutes for our supper, we were sorry that the University had forsworn the opportunity to build one of the airy spacious cafeterias that we found on so many campuses. The stale marmalade on the tables at breakfast next morning had all the evocative significance of Proust's madeleine for the Oxford man.

At Harvard, moreover, there is a college system in operation, similarly an artificial creation since the traditions of the various houses date back only to the 1920s. Their intake is controlled by computers whose aim is to produce an equilibrium of social, athletic and scholastic virtues. The advantage of this mimicry is evident in the standards of comfort in some of the student quarters. Here it is the imaginary rather than the real Oxford that is copied in lavish suites, "The Oxford of the Hollywood movies", as one student neatly put it. It is not merely in architecture and structure that the New World pays homage to the Old. One Oxford expatriate currently attending his law school said that his every word was noted down by Anglodolatrous graduates. One day he asked the Professor sotto voce permission to go to the lavatory, and was rewarded by the sight of the whole class indulging in a buzz of speculation as to what gem had fallen from his English lips.

Ivy League universities cultivate their own special idiosyncrasies. Oxbridge has produced the *Beyond the Fringe* team and *Private Eye*. At Harvard the satire magazine, the *Harvard Lampoon*, possesses a whole building to itself. Yale, we were told, is the only college where the campus newspaper has a gossip column. Certainly we never saw one anywhere else. The very collegiate clothing style in America is called Ivy League. Indeed at conservative Yale the students are presentable enough in their appearance to justify the great herds of male model recruiters who attend their commencement each year disguised as well-meaning uncles. (Or was this arch anecdote of a Michigan State graduate apocryphal? It reveals anyhow the resentments that one kind of student feels for the other.) On the other hand, there is a general tendency on the part of many Harvard and Columbia students to be as ill-kept as possible. There is a rule at Harvard that one must wear coat and tie to meals. It does not specify any particular standards from waist downwards, however, and we noticed the esoteric scruffiness of the jeans which contrasted so greatly with the well-fitting herringbone tweeds above. One Ohio State undergraduate was indeed heard to remark somewhat pathetically that "Guys around here are much Ivier than those slobs at Harvard".

The students at Columbia, Penn, Harvard and Yale struck us as much richer than their midwestern counterparts. They are in fact the chief national institutions, and, for example, the offspring of wealthy midwesterners are traditionally educated at Yale. With the students here we could discuss Athens, Paris and Rome; indeed for many the Grand Tour was an annual event. In the Midwest we were lucky if we found people who had visited Chicago. There were traces of real snobbery, name dropping of Rockefellers and Kennedys. At Columbia one of the debaters had been passed over for the presidency of his fraternity, for which he was clearly the most eligible and logical candidate, in favour of a Russian prince. We found too that Ivy League universities spurn with hauteur the idea of debates coaches—not that this notably improved the quality of their debating.

There were more sinister aspects of eastern seaboard culture. At Yale we were placed in a college guest room. "It's lucky you weren't in a house," said our host knowingly, "or you might have got mixed up with a gang-banging." This, it turned out, was a kind of communal copulation with as many as twenty couples sharing the same room. At Columbia we witnessed a still more extraordinary game. As we were walking along by the side of a dormitory we suddenly saw a student being dangled out of one window by a pair of room-mates, while from another window a torchlight was flashed on to his naked posterior, one buttock of which was painted blue. This, it was explained to us, was a "mooning session", the Ivy League version of tag. Instead of catching another player who then becomes "It", one gives him a view of one's nude behind. He then has to display a similar sight to the next "It". What we had seen was a local variation, called, for obvious reasons, blue-mooning. We left the Ivy League colleges, confident at least that they were different from other institutions of higher education.

Our travels took us next to Bates College, Maine, a small Liberal Arts school, where we were met off the aeroplane at Portland by a Bates student who seemed to personify all the virtues of a true scion of Ivy League land. He wore hunting boots and his complexion and gait were similar to those of Squire Western in *Tom Jones;* he shook hands with us in a vice-like grip, gave a hearty, braying laugh and exclaimed in tones of patronising pity "Welcome to New England".

As we drove from Portland Airport to Bates this jovial man of spirit (an accurate description, since he never stopped offering us and consuming himself vodka cocktails from a specially prepared flask) gave us his views on the current political situation. "I abhor both Goldwater and Johnson. . . . I did not think much of Kennedy either, he was just a mob raiser and his status among people who count was zero. . . . In my room I keep a picture of George Washington—it reminds me of the fact that our present leaders are nowhere near greatness. . . . We need a little more humility in our politics. . . . Incidentally, I just can't

62

understand how in England you can tolerate a Conservative Party of such violently left-wing inclinations."

For all his political bombast we took to this character in a big way. He had a great sense of humour and was very well read and knowledgeable about the arts. During the drive he outlined for us plans for the day. We were to be introduced to a speech professor, answer questions at a luncheon of the local Kiwanis and debate in the college chapel that night. Each of these functions was outlined in those unenthusiastic terms which only a true blasé can produce, generally ending with the comment: "And that'll be ghastlee, absolutely ghastlee."

We were duly introduced to the speech professor, who looked a sort of caricature nonagenarian Heath Robinson boffin, with droopy bloodhound eyes, a wisp of white hair and pince-nez spectacles perched precariously on the end of a beaky nose. He was evidently one of the old school academics, since he greeted us with "How do you do, Aitken. How do you do, Beloff" instead of the usual gush of "Hi Mike, hi Johnny" which came after the introductions from most speech professors. In fact, Professor Brooks Quimby was the doyen of American speech professors and later on in the day showed us his fascinating files of past tours that included a snapshot of the young Rab Butler in full tails in the middle of the 1924 expedition.

Meanwhile though, we had to extend our mission to a new environment. We were to be the guests of honour at the weekly lunch of the Auburn-Lewiston Kiwanis club, a kind of New World Rotary group. Our student hosts were clearly apprehensive about our reactions to this ordeal. "Oh my gawd," Squire Western kept saying. "The Kiwa-a-a-a-a-a-nis. Oh gawd." The luncheon was held

63

in the cavernous *salle à manger* of the local YMCA. The Kiwanis turned out to be business men whose weekly meetings produced a feeling of good fellowship amongst them. In case one good fellow should forget the name of another good fellow, they all sported little badges proclaiming name, nickname and profession. "Dave Gutowski . . . Fatso . . . Stockbroker." Luckily we were not made to comply with this custom since Jonathan's aforementioned versatility of profession would have necessitated a dozen or so badges. After a rapid and somewhat tasteless meal a small man came to a microphone and with feverish zeal led the collected gathering in a few club chants. "God Save the Queen" opened the repertoire. We followed this up with the Kiwani drinking song, the Kiwani sweetheart song the Kiwani guest song. The tunes of these songs were in strong primary chords; and the words, quaint and simple, all conveyed a patriotic message. Alas, there was no new member to be initiated that day, and we were unable to sing the famous Kiwani initiation song whose words ran along these lines: "We are the Kiwanis. We are the Kiwanis. Now you are one, you son of a gun, so have some fun, pom, pom." The singing was carried out with great enthusiasm and after all were sweating profusely we were called upon to give our views on the political situation.

This week was apparently International Relations Week, so Michael was allowed to explain Harold Wilson to the assembled company. Then Jonathan unexplained him again. After short speeches a Colonel X, clearly the appointed buddy boy and spokesman of the group, fired a few questions at us, slapping his knee vigorously the while. A good time was had by all, but clearly it was American politics that interested them most and that evening the local newspaper carried a banner headline "British Debaters Predict November Win for Johnson". Even now we remain disbelieving at our own foresight. After the meeting we were presented with Kiwanis Certificates of Appreciation—prophets honoured in another's country. Our student friends were impressed by our evident enjoyment of the whole affair, a brief glimpse at Babbit land. "Why," one exclaimed, "you ought to go to the Lions next. . . . They'll ro-ar-ar-ar-ar-ar-a-r-a-r-a-r-a-r-ar at you." Should our enthusiasm turn out to be skin deep, however, Squire Western invited us to tea to revive us. Tea for him turned out to mean iced dry martinis at 4.30 in the afternoon. "I just couldn't survive without my cocktails," he drawled, "I am the most scungy boozehound." And in his company we spent a very entertaining two days.

After Bates we went to debate at the Massachusetts Institute of Correction. Since our friends from Yale had assured us that this was merely another name for Harvard we were somewhat surprised to discover that it was, in fact, Norfolk Prison, a pioneer centre of penal reform. Its inmates were voluntary transferees from the State jails, whose only qualifications had to be the attainment of a sufficient degree of criminality. This exclusive character marked it out as an Ivy League Prison.

At the airport we were met by a hireling of the local television network, whose idea of the perfect interview was to talk to himself. After we had mutely assented to the proposition that we greatly looked forward to visiting the Institution and had high hopes of being able to leave it, mutely dissented from the proposition that there was nothing in common between the natives of Norfolk and the natives of Oxford, and mutely consigned our tormentor

65

to the seventh circle of Dante's Inferno, we were driven off in a Z (or as they would pronounce it "Zee") car towards our destination.

It was, we confess (or at least Michael confesses), with a certain amount of trepidation that we prepared ourselves for the debate. Although no one educated at Eton sees anything odd in living behind bars, our knowledge of etiquette on the "inside" was scanty. Should we, for example, pretend that our audience were free as air? "Oh, they know they're inside all right." How about some jests on their status? "Well, my boys are kinda sensitive. . . ." Tentative inquiries elicited the information that both our opponents were in for crimes of violence; one indeed had shot his sweetheart. Generously Michael made Jonathan a present of the "rape" joke for the evening, feeling modestly that an audience of hardened professionals would regard such amateur criminal pretensions as laughable, rather as members of the MCC would scorn a man who boasted of a half-century hit for his village team. Actually the applause with which the sally was eventually greeted showed that the prisoners were far from incredulous about the story. Evidently the image of Oxford in certain quarters of America is not all that it should be. Jonathan was clearly a little hurt since he believes that all his personal relationships are conducted on a purely voluntary basis.

We passed by the sentries, the searchlights, the looming walls with their fringes of barbed wire, and entered one by one through a massive metal door. A snack was provided by the prison chef, whom we complimented on his cuisine with unnatural vigour, the more so since as he handed us the fruit salad, he informed us that the general opinion was that though we might win the debate we would certainly lose the fight afterwards. To the sound of sonorous music from a giant organ we were led on to a wooden stage, concealed from the audience by a thick green curtain. Our sponsor and chairman, a programme informed us, was in charge of the prison arts, entertainment and religion. The organ music appeared to place our debate in the third category of his promotions.

After a few minutes in which we fidgeted and sweated, what seemed to be the entire contents of Congress Library were wheeled in on a trolley, and three prisoners arranged them on the table opposite. The music stopped and the curtain went up. We exchanged mutual glances with the audience. They were segregated into inmates and civilians, one group on either side of the gangway. To our horror we saw among them an old friend, John McDonnell, who had in fact been the Union's last representative on the USA tour. Had he, we wondered, been incarcerated for losing the debate—or, worse still, for winning? At this moment our opponents waltzed on to tremendous cheers from the audience, half of whom were inspired by pride, the other half by fear. Their suave appearance, neat black cardigans, and general look of *bien aise* and cleanliness contrasted with our worn, unshaven greyness. It would have been easy for an outsider to pick out which pair of debaters were the violent criminals.

The resolution that we were to debate that evening was that "The Power of the American Judiciary is Too Great". Thankfully the decision was to be made on the basis of the opinions of the judges and not of the audience, who, we felt, might have been swayed by a certain bias on that particular issue. There is a special technique for prison debates; and it is most important to remember that the

67

stalest joke among free men has an almost unbearable freshness for the prisoner, for whom the clock has stood still since the date of his internment. Jonathan, who is temperamentally suited to prison debates since he has always believed that jokes like wines grow better as they grow older, and who has even been known to repeat a joke told earlier in the evening on the strength of its previous success, commenced in knockabout style. "This is the first time that I have ever had a captive audience; and it is also rare to be speaking opposite men who have the courage of their convictions." After all had recovered their breath some half hour later, the debate proceeded along its usual lines. Our opponents were extremely well read in the subject—they had after all more time at their disposal than most teams—and though we carried the day it was a close decision. One judge, infected by the criminal atmosphere, awarded us eighty points, the Norfolk team seventy-nine, and then the verdict to the latter!!

After the debate we attended a reception, whose enjoyment was only marred when John McDonnell (who turned out to be on a purely voluntary visit from nearby Harvard) asked some of the prisoners whether they had heard him two years previously, which, for men serving a life sentence, was not a wholly tactful question. Our feelings on the evening were best summed up by the Abbé Sièyes who, when asked what he had done during the French Revolution, replied "I survived".

5

Tales from the Old Midwest

FOR THOSE who believe that air travel is a matter of glossy
silver giants powered by a quartet of thunderous jet
engines, of expensive meals straight from the pages of
Robert Carrier served by hostesses straight from the pages
of *Vogue*, of unfailing courtesy and dreamlike smoothness,
the American internal airways in the Midwest come as a
rude awakening. True, there are advantages. Between
towns, where no railway has ever been seen, and whither
no highway runs, aeroplanes travel as the crow flies—that
is to say some twelve feet above the ground with wings
flapping wildly. We sampled no less than fifteen different
airways, each of which had its own little empire. Comparisons are odious—and the reader will have to rely on the
scarcely less odious description.

American airways, we soon discovered, have bred their
own mythology, The modernisation that is so evident in
every terrestrial gadget has not reached the air, and the
airways' fleets consist of small twin-engined planes, referred
to by the affectionate and evocative titles of "goony
birds" and "puddle jumpers". Such is the terror that they
inspire in the breast of every land-bound Yankee that we
half expected to see people cross themselves as these birds

69

of ill-omen flew by—that is after they had ducked first. Everywhere that we went our hosts had their personal anecdotes to regale us with: of engines that had failed; of doors that had dropped off; of runways that had been missed. When we arrived the day before Thanksgiving at Ball State Teachers' Training College, Muncie, Indiana, the debates coach told us that last time he had travelled by that particular route (and it had been for obvious reasons many years ago) the plane had run into a thunderstorm, and after a half-hour of plunging and plummeting the pilot had staggered through the door out of the cockpit, thrown up his hands, burst into tears, exclaimed "I can't take any more of this" and was promptly sick. Fortunately his co-pilot, a man of stouter heart and stomach, had brought them safely in. In view of our own experiences the only part of this encouraging tale that struck us as unlikely was that the plane should have carried a second pilot.

In one way there was an improvement on international transport. To board the plane one could arrive virtually at any time before take-off, and the accomplished athlete could probably arrive even after. Against this had to be set the rigorous rules on baggage allowance. There was no way in which, as on some lenient international airways, one could count as hand baggage anything that one could physically carry on to the plane. The test here was whether or not an item could be taken on board without the use of one's hands. Michael, whose devotion to his growing library of paperbacks was quite touching, would waddle precariously on to the plane, swollen in his three pairs of socks, four sweaters, jacket, two coats, swimming trunks, shorts, trousers, slippers and galoshes, each garment itself

70

stuffed with the best American bookstands have to offer. Jonathan, who preferred to lose dollars rather than dignity, would remonstrate each time with the weigher-in and threaten to report the whole matter to the British Consul. After a while he discarded this successful gambit in favour of the more risky but equally fruitful one of saying that he *was* the British Consul. Finally, some sophisticated label changing in the gentlemen's lavatory in the Pan-Am building at Kennedy Airport crowned the months of manoeuvre with a transatlantic charge evasion.

The interiors of the planes were dark and peeling; and the seats tilted back at an alarming angle since they followed the line at which the plane stood to the ground. The hostesses would sit at the back, usually knitting in an unconcerned manner. For some reason they reminded us of the tricoteuses by the guillotine. On one airline there appeared to be only male stewards. One could see the idea. There are some jobs that are too hair-raising for a mere woman to attempt. After we had fastened our seat belts, we would calculate on our timetables the length of time till the next scheduled descent. Sometimes this would appear as about five minutes. Though this would coincide with our personal estimates of how long the plane could remain airborne, it seemed to us that no company could afford such uneconomical distances. It was not for some while that we realised that there was a time line across which we frequently flew in both directions. With our pilots we rarely came into contact. There were few of those reassuring messages to which the international passenger is accustomed. The only time we were ever aware that there was a pilot in the cabin was on a flight to Boston when a few indistinct and muffled oaths came across the

71

loudspeaker followed by the words, "Don't tell those damned passengers but I can't see a thing in this damned snow".

Coffee or coke is the usual extent of the cuisine on these routes. Once we were offered some sandwiches which dated like the aircraft itself back to the 1930s. It is anyhow not advisable to sample these culinary delights, since all planes on these routes ought to bear a label on their windows saying "I've got a kangaroo in my tank". The altitudes at which they fly makes them vulnerable to the slightest air movement and in addition most of the navigators have all the instincts of failed kamikazi pilots, waiting to dive until almost directly above the port of call, and then swooping down in a vertiginous bolt. On such occasions we would amuse ourselves by inventing famous last words should one of us by some stroke of fortune survive the other's untimely demise.

What struck us with great frequency was how much better travelled inside America we were than the great majority of the American students that we met. Americans think nothing of travelling fifteen miles for a beer; fifty miles for a dinner; a hundred miles for a debate; and still greater distances for more personal amusements. Yet even these exertions cannot take them more than a fraction of the way across their home State; and the result is that to the inhabitants of Bowling Green, Ohio, New York seems as far away as Paris. It is often forgotten that "provincialism" is just as apparent a phenomenon in America as it is in England. The feeling of a "common culture" that we had enjoyed with the debonair sophisticates of the Atlantic seaboard vanished as we now plunged into jungle America, whither, it swiftly appeared, few Englishmen had ever travelled before. East Coast is East Coast and Midwest is Midwest, and never the twain shall meet.

We soon got into the rhythm of travel. We would fly into a little airport, carved out of a sprawling field, and disembark as casually as if we were leaving a bus. After a few minutes all the locals would have hurried away, and we would be left in splendid isolation by the luggage counter. We would discuss for a quarter-of-an-hour whether to phone the college and announce our arrival (the predictable arrival of "winter-time" had knocked most of our schedules sideways) or to find our own way there. Usually at our moment of decision a small group who had been standing at the other end of the hall would bear down on us and say:

"Are you the guys from England? We recognised you *at once*. Say, though, is Aitken going to wear his fancy dress for the debate tonight?" This oft-repeated opening gambit was the result of the identification pictures that all the speech professors had. In the middle of May we had supplied photographs to the Institute at twenty-four hours' notice, little realising that the choices of a thoughtless moment were to be plastered across the notice boards of half a century of campuses from Maine to Michigan to Mississippi. Jonathan had been snapped in full evening tails just before a Union debate. Michael had excavated a shot of himself in a heavy polo necked sweater. The Midwesterners were fascinated by this difference in attire which they imagined was merely typical of the distinct ways in which the British Conservative and the British Socialist always dressed; a kind of modern version of the top hat versus cloth cap war.

After this we would be questioned on our identity.

Jonathan had immediate status as a relative of Lord Beaverbrook. Michael achieved less eminence as the putative son of Hilaire Belloc, and after the General Election his prestige sunk to zero as he was invariably cast as the offspring of the nefarious Tommy Balogh. What was more, Jonathan had actually met the Beatles. The fact that this brief encounter had taken place in the lavatory in an Oxford pub in no way diminished the awe in which he was held. Teenage girls used in fact to touch him as if he were some mediaeval monarch whose benediction would remove the scrofula. Michael, who had once been to a dance at which the Rolling Stones had played, was again hopelessly outclassed.

We would be deposited in our hotel, motel, or guest house and given a couple of rest hours until dinner. All the hotel rooms had baths, radios, room service and television sets. Once, in fact, we were charged half price simply because the television set didn't work. At about half-past-five we would be fetched and taken to the evening meal with an escort of faculty dignitaries and giggling dates. Americans eat their meals in a looking-glass way. First of all large cups of coffee are brought on. Next one is presented with a piece of rainbow-coloured jelly nestling in a lettuce leaf. After that one has salad. Then the pièce de résistance, the gargantuan slab of rare roast beef. And finally a sherry on the rocks. We decided that the best feature of American cuisine was the merits of the cheap food. We use the word "cheap" in no absolute sense but merely to denote "less expensive than expensive" food. The fact that the drugstore hamburger costs little less than a steak at the Savoy Grill in no way detracts from the fact that it is difficult to go far wrong with an American sandwich or hot dog. Once indeed, over a period of four days, we became exclusive patrons at the Trailways Café de Transport in Gainesville, Florida, where we ate six successive meals. A similar exercise at a British Railways restaurant would probably chop years off one's life. The only thing that the ignorant traveller should beware is the volatile meaning that such words as "large" and "small" denote on an American menu. In a restaurant near Duke University in South Carolina Jonathan had a memorable experience of this. We all decided to have pizzas, the *spécialité de la maison;* and Jonathan with good appetite ordered a "large" one. His apprehension was aroused when the waiter arrived with the pizzas for the other diners, fragrant spiced pastries with a circumference that lapped at the edges of the plate. A moment after two more waiters hove into view, sweating beneath a concoction en ronde about the size of the Rose Window at Chartres. Even our hosts' genial invitation to "tie on the feedbags" failed to inspire Jonathan to complete this particular enterprise.

In some of the more remote campuses an Englishman was as much of an oddity as a Martian, and we got used to being treated by some of the students more as specimens than as visitors. But as Englishmen we had a certain prestige. At Murray State University, Kentucky, Jonathan was assigned the task of telephoning his host's date, informing her that he had learnt to speak English as the English spoke it, and "proving" his new and valued accomplishments by whispering anglicised endearments at her to an accompaniment of melting sighs from the other end of the wire.

"The guys from Oxford" were a popular sideshow on and off the stage; and if we found something rather sinister in such questions as "Do English boys ever go out with girls?" that one seeker after truth posed to us at Edinboro Teachers' Training College, Pennsylvania, we were impressed with the curiosity that was always shown. The Beatles were the prime topic of concern. Indeed, if we'd been paid a dime for every time we were asked our opinion about the talents of that harmonious, if hairy, quartet, we would have become almost as rich as they are. Questions on the National Health Service ran second; on the Queen third; with a canvass for our views on American maidenhood and Barry Goldwater in a photo-finish for fourth place. Only occasionally did we stumble across evidence of startling ignorance about our mother country. One air hostess, detecting our origins in our accents, proceeded to inform us that "If you come from England, you must know my friends Betsy and Bugsy Bookbinder . . . ", and seemed quite shocked when we told her that England's population was now in the region of sixty million inhabitants. And at Ohio State University the parent of one of our hosts was overheard to say to his wife "Oxford? Isn't that where President Kennedy went to college?" "No, dear. That was Harvard." But no doubt both were equally beyond his ken.

One phenomenon that was common to campuses throughout the Midwest was the single Oxford expatriate. Typically this figure would have spent a year at Regent's Park College or the Department of Education during the war. He would wear with the pride of a uniform a dark blue blazer, resplendent with University crest and a 1920 pair of Oxford bags. On the wall would hang an oar purloined from a member of the famous Christ Church crew of 1935 and glossy photographs of the Department

Shove Ha'penny Team after their annual dinner. His
conversation was endless reminiscence based on a better
than average knowledge of every pub within three square
miles of Tom Quad. He would subscribe to the *Weekly
Guardian*, mourn an unfinished thesis on "The Political
Philosophy of Ortega", and bore the pants off us in a
quick half-hour. It was considered obligatory that we
should meet these quaint characters with their alma mater
fixation and anyone with the slightest claims to educational
kinship was called upon to provide a soirée. "You must
meet Hank," they said to us at Monmouth. "He's been to
Oxford, Cambridge and places of that kind."

We were, in fact, a little flattered by the attention paid
to making us feel at home. At the University of Pittsburgh
our old friend the Speech Professor Bob Newman, who had
spent a sabbatical at Oxford the previous summer, staged
a full style "Parliamentary" debate for us in the middle of
the afternoon. Michael's partner, an emigré Austrian
socialist with an unpronounceable name and the faintest
trace of blond hair on his upper lip, was dignified with the
title of the "Honourable Member from Vienna"; and all in
all they did the fifty-first state proud. At Hanover College,
Indiana, at the end of a debate on "Politics is Far Too
Serious a Matter for Intellectuals" the speech professor
got up and made a little speech in honour of the fact that
it was the ninetieth birthday of Sir Winston Churchill,
whose career, he diplomatically added, "provided such a
deal of evidence for both sides of the resolution". Everywhere too we were offered tea to drink, a beverage de-
nounced by Michael as "suitable only for vicars and char-
ladies". Once indeed at Wisconsin State College, Whitewater, where the speech department is run by a matriarchy,

77

we were invited to a tea-tasting ceremony, conducted in high ritual, where six different sorts of tea were produced, their bouquets inhaled, their vintages analysed—and we regaled ourselves on Chateau Red Label 1963.

We progressed in somewhat uneven direction across the Midwest from Pennsylvania to Ohio to Wisconsin to Michigan to Indiana. One of the first stops on our schedule was Mount Mercy College, Pittsburgh, where we were to debate the motion "Frailty, Thy Name is Woman". This provided us with a welcome light interlude and we were eager indeed to get to grips with it. We arrived in Pittsburgh by Greyhound, and were greeted by a sallow and suspicious-looking figure who appeared to be chaperoning his two charges, both of whom we noted were girls. We exchanged significant glances—for our jests, though we would have hesitated to call them in bad taste, at least recognised that there were differences between the two sexes—that is, all except those jokes (which maybe were in bad taste) which failed to recognise these differences. Evidently there would have to be some minor operation on our speeches to temper them to the innocent minds of our partners. What we were not prepared for was to perform major surgery in two hours flat; and only when our driver informed us that "Sister Ursula was so looking forward to what you have to say to our young girls" did it dawn on us that we were to debate in a convent. Michael was particularly sensitive about this revelation, since the previous year he had told an audience at the Hemel Hempstead Arts Festival a joke about a one-legged nun called Hopalong Chastity, and five minutes later a female in black had limped ostentatiously out of the back of the room. That evening he had intended to begin his speech "Jonathan Aitken was born

78

under Virgo. . . . The biggest single blow the science of astrology has ever received. He spends his evenings sowing his wild oats and wakes up praying for crop failure. He is, too, well known for his chevalerie—a French word meaning 'Horseplay'!" Jonathan by way of reiteration had planned to start: "Michael Beloff is well known for his taste in fast cars and fast women. For this reason he is known as Oxford's Alfa Romeo. I heard two of Mike's girl friends discussing him once. 'Doesn't he dress well?' said the first. 'Yes,' replied the other, 'and quickly too.' " On the way across in the coach we had practised these bons mots on each other and had been interrupted by a Negro fellow traveller with a "Remember, man. There's women on this bus".

We spent a frenzied couple of hours converting our material into such as would pass the censorship of the strictest of critics, and were heartened to see that our efforts had not been in vain, since the first four rows were solid in black habit. They were informed now that "Jonathan, a pious and gentle youth, is not at all prejudiced on the subject. Indeed some of his best friends are women." They tittered with delight to hear that "Michael has met the only girl in the world for him—no less than twelve times." We spoke of Madame Curie, Jane Austen, Mamie Eisenhower; and Jonathan recounted a short parable whose theme was that charity beats chastity by a short head, but only just. The girls were sharp and witty and although not immune to the American debaters' disease of building their speeches out of the brick and straw of statistic and quotation, were themselves eloquent disproof of the truth of the motion. After the debate we had a variety of questions fired at us.

"What sort of a girl would you like to marry?" "A girl like you"—oh gallant Jonathan.

"What do you think of American girls?" "Beautiful, intelligent, well mannered and charming. Can I meet you alone afterwards?"—a quick riposte by Michael.

And so on, Gilbert Harding-ing our way into the night.

Two days later we were back in Pittsburgh, and after a three o'clock debate, and a generously protracted cocktail party, our hosts escorted us—it was October 29th, five days before the Presidential election—to hear Barry Goldwater at a rally in the city's Civic Arena.

1964 was the year that the Republicans became America's largest minority party. Led by fighter pilot Barry ("In your guts, you know he's nuts") and William Miller—christened by us "Elephant Bill", the GOP suffered landslide defeat at the hands of the Democrats. They said that if the Republicans put up a yellow dog for President, he'd poll forty million votes. Barry got thirty-seven million. As the 1964 election fades in the memory, and the emotions of the time are buried under the statistics of psephologists, people may forget exactly what Goldwater stood for, exactly what were the responses that he struck from his supporters. It is important that people don't forget, for the election was not just the best elephant joke of the century.

We arrived two hours before the meeting started, but were nevertheless the last allowed in. Civil Rights supporters circled around the building singing the freedom anthem "We shall overcome", under the eyes of the ubiquitous vigilant policemen. One banner proclaimed with possibly prophetic optimism "Come on, GOP. Scranton and Romney in 1968". Another—less prophetic but more optimistic—said "Young Republicans love Ringo". Inside the arena the auditorium was alive with flags, hats, badges and banners. In England one would have thought it was a Cup Tie audience. Quick to seize on the recent scandals (it seemed to us that American politicians never hit above the belt where below will do), vast sheets hung over the sides of the tiers advising "Keep our Mens Rooms Safe" and "Walt Jenkins is LBJ's Profumo". "The choice is Barryland or Fairyland." Spotlights picked out the stage as at a theatre and a loudspeaker dangled like a giant spider from the concave ceiling. In the interval before the show started collection boxes were handed round, and pamphlets passed from hand to hand. These varied from the lunatic to the absurd. One purported to be a biography of Hubert Humphrey, that well-known "Marxist Socialist". A convincing case was presented to justify this description. He had, for example, visited Poland! Moscow Radio was said to have welcomed his candidature. Worst of all, he was known to be a supporter of the United Nations, that "Red Front Organisation". For those of the Goldwater apostles who could not read (or could not read much) there was a photograph of Humphrey on the front of the pamphlet with political sidekick Orville Freeman, captioned "Power hungry Humphrey celebrates a recent political victory. *Note the clenched fist.*" Another broadsheet insinuated that Bobby Kennedy had been a paramour of the late Marilyn Monroe, who had of course been a Communist agent. Her tragic suicide, it was obliquely suggested, was no suicide at all—but a cover-up job by the FBI. Finally, a newspaper called *Liberty* carried the headline "The Truth about LBJ", and contained a story of several thousand words that implicated the President in every Texan political scandal that had happened since the first World War, in several that had not happened, and threw in a few hints at sexual perversion and hired murder as well. It all made the "Bonkers" broadside seem very small beer. We could never understand why it was that American newspapers made so much play with the heckling in the British election. It was a little like the Mafia getting hot under the collar because of the Mods and Rockers.

At 7.30 pm the build-up began. "Land of the Free" was played on an organ. We were then invited to pray. The priest broke all Thomas à Becket's records for political involvement. It was less a prayer than a preach-in. The Bible was quoted as if it had been expressly written to refute *Das Kapital*. "Give us, O Lord, our daily bread, but not from the subsidised farms. . . . Lead us out of the bondage into which the Federal Government has placed us. . . . O Lord who divided the sons of Ham from the sons of Shem and Japhet. . . ." The prayer reached a crescendo "Give us, O Lord, a hot line to heaven and not a hot line to the Godless in the Kremlin"; at which point God intervened, showing himself a good Democrat, by sabotaging the loudspeaker equipment—and the remainder of the prayer was simply a one-man puppet show. Politics and religion now departed from the stage and made way for entertainment. Cabaret; singers; jugglers; and a long line of "Manhattan Rockettes", dancing girls whose stirring high kicks somewhat belied the note of Puritanism that underlay the Republican message of 1964.

The crowd was of all ages (physically, not mentally) but there was a high proportion of bobbysoxers. No Democrats (these were disciples, not doubters), no Negroes— we thought that we and our hosts were the only people in

the audience who didn't think that Barry Goldwater was
the biggest thing to hit America since Davy Crockett.
Michael even saw a real genuine bona-fide old lady in
tennis shoes complain to her companion, "I don't understand the way the world is today".

Some ageing star from the golden era of Hollywood was
now pushed to the front of the stage (to judge from his
powers of oratory, one would guess that his speciality had
been mime or tap-dancing) to give the view of man in the
motorways on what was wrong with contemporary America.
His acute analysis of American history started in 1932, the
year the rot set in. Since then apparently social security,
unemployment benefits, fluoridisation, and the perverts
and commies who ran the mass media had been sapping
the American strength and undermining the American
conscience. "LBJ wants to take from the haves and to give
to the have nots. Americans should do things for themselves." Cheers split the air. After a frantic peroration in
which he advocated all-out war on East Germany he was
shuffled off the stage, to a few sonorous chords from the
organ.

Americans believe in grass roots politics. For them the
democratic process involves electing every local official,
be he of the judiciary, legislature, or executive—and preferably together. As if we were at a school prize giving, for
the next half-an-hour candidates for every conceivable
office came up from their seats in the orchestra pit for a
brief moment of personal glory at the rostrum, where they
were introduced, cheered and sent back into the obscurity
from which they had emerged. By now the audience had
been titivated to the point of political orgasm. Even the
introduction of a man with a billboard saying "By their

83

fruits shall they be known. And the fruits of Lyndon Johnson are Bobby Baker and Billy Sol Estes" failed to satisfy them. There were great growls of "We want Barry. . . . We want Barry", accompanied by stamping, clapping, rattle waving and clinking of the collection boxes. As handsome Governor Bill Scranton emerged into the spotlight there were ugly shouts. Here was Judas trying to make it up with Jesus. An honest speech, in which Scranton admitted to continuing differences with Goldwater, but pledged himself to work loyally for a Republican victory in November, was greeted with further catcalls. A short glimpse of Peggy Goldwater (Madame du Barry) and then the hero, silver-haired, erect, smiling, strode to the microphone.

There followed no less than nineteen minutes of solid cheering, which made a Beatles reception look like the applause for a minor cabinet minister at a Tory women's tea-party. It was startling and terrifying. After we had heard Goldwater speak, we guessed that the motive was less enthusiasm at his appearance than desire to prevent him opening his mouth. This was wishful thinking. There was hysteria in the Pittsburgh Civic Arena that night, and it was enough to worry any small "d" democrat. What Goldwater said was unimportant; the usual farrago of innuendo about White House morals, attacks on a weak foreign policy (there were clearly many Eastern European emigrés in the audience because banners demanding the freeing of Hungary, Poland, etc., proliferated), fears for American freedom in face of government activity.

Michael was all the time taking notes for a dispatch to the *Evening Standard*. After a while he noticed that he was being watched by a group of teenagers, who were crowded

84

behind him. "Are you a spy?" one of them, an attractive fresh-faced brunette, asked him. "No," he replied, "I'm doing a report for the London *Evening Standard*." "Is that a pinko paper like the *Pittsburgh Evening Gazette?*" (This newspaper currently favoured the Democratic cause.) "No," said Michael, the memory of Lord Beaverbrook sustaining him in the belief that he was telling the truth. "That's all right, you can stay then!" This was encouraging news, though Michael felt a note of menace. Clearly his credentials were not above suspicion. Sure enough, five minutes later, the appointed spokesman returned to the investigation. "Isn't it a tragedy about what happened to poor Douglas-Home in England?" The cock was crowing thrice. "No," Michael replied. "Actually it's a very good thing." Gasp. Then as if by some bush telegraph we heard the message whispered through the crowd. "A socialist, a socialist, a socialist." There was evidently a debate between those who wished to expel Michael and those who wished to convert him. The doves won. "We don't want any of that stuff here," young Miss Republican said. Michael nodded gingerly. "Have you read *1984?*" My God, Michael thought, is that a crime too? "Yes." "If we don't have Goldwater, that's what'll happen to America." Michael's failure to grasp the full implications of the Goldwatery mentality is revealed by the fact that he thought that this meant that the soft-on-Communism foreign policy would lead to Russian invasion, and the establishment of Soviet dictatorship in God's own country. But no! When Goldwater, in one of his finer moments, referred to the ethics of "Big Brother", Michael's political instructress nudged him and whispered "LBJ". Evidently the mild form of state capitalism and welfareism that prevailed

85

in America in 1964 was seen by these young people as the prologue to the establishment of an omnicompetent Leviathan.

Meanwhile, Jonathan had inveigled his way to the Press bench. "Where are you from?" demanded the reporter from the *Los Angeles News*. "England," Jonathan replied. "Have you come here to pervert the truth?" This was a remark that it was impossible to answer. The journalist then turned to political issues. "How long are Wilson and his gang of Redskis going to stay in power?" There was no absolutely obvious reply to this. Having launched his few remarks in the cause of freedom, the reporter turned to the compilation of his record of the gospel according to St Barry. Thirty minutes later the meeting ended; and stunned, disbelieving, we emerged into the cool Pittsburgh night.

"I bet you haven't got anyone like Barry in England," Michael's young Republican friend said to him in an ecstatic swoon. "No," he replied with conviction, "no."

Fortunately to our way of thinking and to that of sixty-two per cent of Americans, Goldwater did not win the election. On the great night we were at Hiram College, Ohio, and the debates coach invited us over to watch the results coming in on the screen. We sat around smoking cigars and drinking tinned sodas and watched Gulf Oil advertisements for three hours. At 7.31 pm with a fraction of one per cent of the votes counted, the NBS computers announced a Democrat landslide—a truly remarkable illustration of machine intelligence, since mere human beings had come to the same conclusion some eight weeks previously. By midnight it appeared that there was no need to go underground for at least another four years, and so we went to bed instead.

Ohio was the first state where we spent a full weekend; and we were able to satisfy our curiosity about the way in which the American spends the Sabbath.

In Britain, America has the reputation of being a God-fearing nation. We are told that sixty-five per cent of the population of the United States are regular churchgoers compared to four per cent in Britain. Republican and Democrat politicians refer to past and future guidance from the Almighty with a frequency that their British counterparts would find embarrassing. Even in the world of pop singers, Pat Boone gives half his income to his religion, Elvis Presley now makes half his income from singing about religion and Dr Billy Graham draws bigger crowds than both of them. British preachers declaim from their pulpits the degeneracy of Anglo-Saxon youth compared to the purity of American adolescents. Religion, it seems, looms really large on the other side of the Atlantic.

We found little evidence that this pious choir-boy image extended to the universities.

The first, and last, adventure into the field of religion was made by Jonathan. The debates coach at the university where we were week ending interrupted our Sunday morning slumber by breezing into our room remarking "You're coming to Church, aren't you?" Since he weighed twenty stone and was armed with a menacingly bulky prayer book it seemed unwise to demur from what was obviously intended as a statement of fact, and so Jonathan assented.

The church of the debates coach's choice was in the local town a mile away from the campus. "It's the only good one in these parts," he remarked knowingly, indicating that in his opinion there was something inherently evil about the Catholic, Methodist and Anglican establishments that had been passed by on the other side. We halted outside what looked like a solid lugubrious bank on which was perched a rather stumpy turret topped with a flag pole and generously described as a spire. One of the neighbourhood's poor and needy was employed as a twentieth-century good shepherd in directing limousines to appointed spaces in the car park. He was doing smart business accepting commissions to wash automobiles while their devout owners were going about the Lord's business within.

The turreted slab of white concrete which Jonathan had originally thought was a bank turned out really to be the church itself. On close inspection the only sign of external holiness was a blue neon sign which glowed sanctimoniously with the words "Assembly of Christ". These were replaced every ten seconds with a brief flash in red neon "Come inside". On accepting this invitation Jonathan was ushered along a luxurious thick pile carpet into the church and was shown into a pew marked with the notice "Reserved for visitors from Oxford, England". In order that their guests should not feel lonely in this isolated splendour ten members of the Missionary Committee (the Assembly of Christ's closest link to foreign relations) entered the pew, each one shaking hands with the visitor from Oxford and murmuring reverently the phrase "Glad to know you, Mr Aitken".

The pews in American Churches are designed for comfort. They have to be, for the role of a worshipper in the United States is entirely sedentary. If he wishes to pray he sits forward on the foam rubber cushions, and if he is exceptionally devout bows his head in his hands. In order to sing hymns he merely sits upright and in order to listen to the sermon he reclines backwards (and sometimes falls asleep). All of this seems very strange, since both the Church of England and the Church of Rome keep their congregations in a state of perpetual motion, bobbing up and down on every possible pretext.

As Jonathan snuggled comfortably into the velvet encased foam rubber pew, he noticed what looked like a small machine equipped with knobs and dials and wheels at the head of the pew. He asked a member of the Missionary Committee what it was, and received the answer, "It's for the bread and wine," and with this he had to be content until communion service began. The preliminaries to the communion service were unexciting. The congregation leant forward to pray for guidance for their responsibilities in the coming election, they leant back to hear the sermon on responsibilities of the citizen in voting, and sat upright to join in jolly anthems about the harvest. The choir was presided over by an elderly middle-aged matron whose voluminous white surplice had attached to it by the shoulders two golden strips of cardboard which were evidently meant to represent angel's wings. These creaked noisily as she athletically conducted the choir, thus marring an otherwise admirable musical performance.

When the solemn moment of the Holy Sacrament arrived two gentlemen emerged from the back of the church carrying with them large white strips of canvas which they attached to the wheels placed beside every pew. It became evident that a gigantic conveyor belt was being fixed up, and at a signal from the Minister the machinery went into action and trays of iced red wine were lifted from the altar on to the conveyor belt which then lifted them to each pew. Each of these big trays contained twelve thimblefuls of iced wine and twelve cellophane wrapped individual biscuits. With a great crackling of paper and throbbing of the conveyor belt, not to mention a rendering of ghostly electronic music from an organist who had evidently learnt his trade at Hollywood cinemas showing horror films, we partook of the Last Supper. It was certainly the last time that Jonathan would go near the Assembly of Christ.

As the month of November wore on, and we wore out, we began to look forward to the haven of Thanksgiving. Our last but one stop was at Wabash College, Indiana, where we witnessed the famous Wabash beanie fight, another example of American tribal rites. All the freshmen at Wabash College have to wear small caps or "beanies" for their first semester to make clear their inferior status to any who might be ignorant of it. But at the end of the semester they are given an opportunity to rid themselves of this indignity. A beanie is placed at the top of a fifteen-foot high pole which is liberally covered with lashings of glutinous grease. The sophomores, guardians of the sacred relic, stand around the pole in defence; and the freshmen charge at them and try to remove the beanie. Since this entails constructing a human pyramid three stories high in conflict with grease and energetic sophomore alike the task is a difficult one. They are allowed three tries of four minutes each. There was already the chill of dusk in the air; and the sight of these sweating and often bloody bodies was not a pleasant one. The inhabitants of the town watched their so-called betters in wonderment from behind the confines of a fence. For one unfortunate an ambulance was called; we had no doubt that doctors awaited others.

The whole affair was a cross between the Eton Wall Game and an early gladiatorial contest, and one of the teachers refused to send his son to the college, as he was so disgusted by it. When we asked our hosts why this barbarity persisted they said, "We had to do it—and we're not going to stop it for them"—a good American reason.

The next day we flew into Muncie, Indiana, well known across the USA as the end of the world. It was a day of relentless rain—and all that we succeeded in doing was in attracting the lowest audience of our tour. In the auditorium were seventeen people, ten of whom were members of one of the debater's family, three of whom were high-school children curious to see real English people, and four of whom were members of the local John Birch Society who had come to hear us lay into the liberal perverts of the Supreme Court. The first two categories were doubtless contented with the show, though not the third.

As we drove back to the home of the apologetic debates coach, he pointed out to us the flag poles that decorated the front garden of every house. "You can tell this is good John Birch territory," he said. "They only lower flags on two occasions: if a President's assassinated or if their dog dies. They're always on at me to censor the students' textbooks for being unpatriotic. What with that and the fundamentalist lobby who say that the books are ungodly and that they deny the teachings of the Bible, I have a hard time getting anyone to learn anything." Unfortunately we were unable to meet any of his oppressed pupils, for everyone had gone home for Thanksgiving. For weeks now we had seen on each central campus noticeboard notices with captions such as "Three people wanted to share cost of gas for car to Washington, Seattle" out of which protruded little hooks on which were looped rings with names of eager applicants. So in an orgy of mutual help the student population of America sped homewards.

6

Sex and the Single Student

SEX IS the most popular of the extra curricular activities on the American campus. It is discussed, analysed, argued over, and sometimes even practised. We doubt, though, that it is ever fully enjoyed, for the beacon of passion is shrouded in a fog of verbal profundity and careful planning which seems to surround every amorous advance. If a student has an interest in sex at all, he is condemned to unrelieved tedium, for the life of vice and the life of virtue go equally unrewarded.

Those who pursue the road that leads to the altar do so with all the stern intensity of two senior wranglers working out an arithmetical progression. Self-appointed Kinseys of the Campus, we started our researches in a vaulted hall in Denison, Ohio, where we were the visiting speakers at a seminar held for the local Sunday school (age group 8–12). These cradle Casanovas were swift to divert the dialogue into inappropriate channels. Dating begins at the age of ten, we were authoritatively informed. Evidence of pre-adolescent use of lipstick we could see for ourselves. "The only trouble is," one scornful infant sneered, "the girls have to wear padding."

A single date is risky; a second date can be a near disaster.

93

One English boy, whom we met in Urbana, Illinois, had a cautionary tale for us. Having spent a mere two (and chaste) evenings in the company of an American maiden, he had been taken home and presented over the festive hamburger as someone who, if he had not actually proposed to the girl in question, was nevertheless a man of wholly honourable intentions. It was not that our friend had had dishonourable intentions. He had had no intentions at all. But then the path of American love is like a bobsleigh run. Once you're embarked, there is virtually no way of getting off.

If a couple have dated two or three times they are then regarded as "going steady". And a few months later they become "pinned".

Getting pinned did not, to our surprise, mean getting pinned down or pinned together; in university circles it meant that the man handed over his fraternity pin to his would-be spouse of four years hence to signify that the couple were engaged to be engaged. Since, however, many worthies, including Jews, Negroes, Infidels and other men of good breeding do not usually get elected to fraternities, yet suffer still this strange transatlantic urge, a system has been devised whereby you can get into the pinned category by exchanging tie pins, coat pins, hat pins or even safety pins.

It is a very significant step to get pinned. Thenceforth you cannot go out with any member of the opposite sex other than your pin-pal. Since pinning takes place between the ages of 16 and 19 it means that from then on love is reduced to canine fidelity. "If my girl went out for an evening with another guy I'd break it off with her," said a freshman from Purdis, Indiana. His attitude was not exceptionally possessive. But then his girl friend was not exceptionally prepossessing.

The most subtle nuances of the American vocabulary of lovers' status are, like the correct use of the imperfect tense in Russian, impossible for the most sensitive foreigner to master. Quite what was meant, for example, when a Columbia graduate described his relationship with his girl friend as being "more than pin" we shall never know. But, more important, we rebelled against the whole notion of hierarchy and we thought the rituals of "going steady" and "pinning" took the romance out of romance. Their widespread practice means that a high proportion of student couples have no understanding whatsoever of members of the opposite sex apart from the one singled out at the age of eighteen by the lottery of adolescent calf love. The social climate enforces these immature gimmicks so that a boy or girl who "unpins" is regarded as a betrayer of good faith. This makes early marriages inevitable and perhaps explains why the American divorce rate is so astonishingly high. We remember well at Florida Presbyterian College our meeting with an attractive brunette of some twenty years, the female escort of one of the debaters, and our surprise at discovering that she was not only a divorcée but also a mother. It added a certain piquancy to the story to discover that her woeful wooer rejoiced in the Christian name of "Randy".

But the outsiders, the Don Juans and James Bonds of the campus, are no better off, for Americans succeed in the astonishing achievement of making immorality and infidelity utterly boring.

There is something very deliberate about promiscuity among the American young. Indeed, the intensity of the

95

strategic calculation and tactical forethought obliterate the romantic spirit of eccentric improvisation which is the starting point of so many Oxford love affairs.

There are certain golden rules to which any aspiring transtlantic Romeo must conform. The first rule is that no amorous advance can take place until after sunset. "A completely new atmosphere comes over the campus when darkness falls," said one Pennsylvanian sophomore. "I guess the boys kinda get braver when no one can see what they're doing." A blasé man about campus in Florida told us, "I never lay my birds before 10 pm—I can't stand long energetic evenings." This contrasts strangely with the way of life in certain Oxford and Cambridge circles, where drawn curtains in women's colleges on hot summer afternoons are viewed with the profoundest suspicion.

The second rule is that all indulgence in sex must, if possible, be preceded by indulgence in alcohol. Drinking is therefore the second most serious extra curricular activity. Detailed planning is required for it since most universities forbid the drinking of alcohol on or in the vicinity of the campus. We frequently found that agreeable October afternoons had to be spent in piling into cars, driving for thirty miles, just for the illicit pleasure of swigging two or three cans of Budweiser beer in some little bolt hole unlikely to be policed by university authorities.

The drinking is systematic rather than hedonistic. For example, one girl we met proudly informed us that she belonged to the Pi Drinking Club whose membership consisted of girls who had taken the momentous pledge not to engage in sexual intercourse until their escorts had bought them approximately seven double bourbons. Others we met were described as being "three beer girls". We didn't meet those who did it just on one bottle of Coca Cola but no doubt they exist.

Because alcohol is prohibited on most campuses it acquires a mystique and attraction which it would never have were it readily available. Oxford, with its fifty-nine public houses within one mile of Carfax, may produce more drunkards, but less time is wasted on nonsensical bibulous rituals which rule out sex for teetotallers.

The third rule to which sex-conscious students conform is that all preliminary advances must be made in a motor-car. This explains the huge size of American automobiles. Car owners who can only afford Fiats and other makes which provide merely bucket seats are at a distinct disad-vantage. One must have a spacious bench-style front seat, preferably with a back which folds down, thus making the entire seating space into a quasi-bed.

We vividly remember passing row after row of parked cars on certain campuses. None of them seemed to have any seats of any inhabitants, but our guides informed us that these stationary vehicles were invariably populated with one, two and sometimes three couples. No wonder America continues to break records in car production, for "A car of their own" is the ambition of all American teenage couples. At Normal, Illinois, we found that one of our Oxford predecessors had left behind him a legendary reputation as an auto-lover who apparently was a master of the clutch but had never known when to put on the brakes. It was only intensive inquiry on our part that excavated this myth and solved to our satisfaction the mystery of our hosts' arcane welcome "Have a Volks, folks!"

The fourth rule is that copulation initially must take

97

place in a motel. Motels are the sin palaces of America. No questions are asked. You drive in, take your key, use your room and drive away.

The only person ever to have had trouble with moral investigations in a motel was Michael. Out on a date he inadvertently found himself far away from campus after midnight, which was curfew hour for women's dormitories. The girl, who had no doubt in true American style been calculating things all along, suggested that she should be provided with accommodation in a nearby motel. Michael's innocent chivalry ran to the sum of nine dollars which he handed over to a female motel clerk, who presented him with a key and a knowing wink which he returned, thinking it to be a local custom among hoteliers.

When he got to the room he found that his key did not fit, and after a long struggle he returned to the reception desk to complain. Subsequent investigation showed that he had been trying to open the door of this motel room with the key of another motel in which the university had booked us. Coughing with embarrassment he pulled out a handkerchief and a third hotel key, absent-mindedly plundered from a stopping place earlier on our tour, clattered to the ground. The receptionist and other female attendants collapsed in paroxysms of giggles and whispers of "Bluebeard" and "Valentino" rang in his ears. The original beneficiary of this hospitality was doubtless all the more astonished at finding herself spending a lonely night.

The final golden rule of campus liaisons is that they must be accompanied by as much publicity as possible. In American sex indiscretion is the better part of valour. Boasting, by both members of the team, is obligatory. We were astonished by the frankness with which male and

98

female students would with relish reveal every detail of their own and other people's private lives.

Twenty-four hours after arriving on American soil, we attended a cocktail party given by a fraternity at Columbia University.

English cocktail parties are renowned for the triviality of their gossip. Questions such as "Do you have a good thing for the National?" or "Did you get honkers at Penny's party last night?" fill the air. At Columbia the conversational approach was more direct. A pretty young thing from fashionable Sarah Lawrence College sidled up to Jonathan and without further ado asked:

"In England do you think it's wrong for a girl to have an affair with a Negro? I'm curious 'cos I'm having one myself."

Jonathan, slow on moral arbitration but quick on compliments, contented himself with the murmur, "Lucky, Negro!"

"No. Lucky me. Once you've been to bed with a Negro, you find white boys just so much seaweed!"

Jonathan politely questioned this oceanic aspersion on white virility, only to be faced with reinforcements. The pretty young thing summoned a friend.

"Martha, tell Jonathan about Sammy."

With spontaneous enthusiasm Sammy's undoubtedly unique abilities between the sheets were described in detail. Martha assured us that all the knowledgeable girls in her dormitory would tell similar tales about their Negro lovers. Oxford must in comparison be a very dull place for girls.

The direct approach to sexual problems was further illustrated by our reception at Denison University, Ohio.

99

Hardly had we stepped off the aircraft and shaken hands with our two-man reception committee when one of them, blinking owlishly from behind what looked like an innocuous pair of spectacles, enquired, "Say, you boys had any sex life lately?" The answer was a regretful "No." Our other host chortled, "Wal, if you're frustrated Toby's the man to fix you up." He was. On the short drive from the airport to our guest room he offered us anything from a one-legged masochist lesbian to a sixty-year-old married woman with a taste for flagellation before midnight and soixante-neuf after it.

It seemed, however, that he was not immediately equipped to deliver the goods and it transpired too that the well-meaning Professor of Debating had decided to furnish us with two blind dates for the evening.

This was our first introduction to the American practice of blind dates. We afterwards concluded that the expression meant that in order to enjoy the date one had to be blind. When our predestined partners appeared it was noted that the dates were not only blind but also dumb.

Feeling like a couple of guide dogs we prepared for the evening's entertainment, which was to consist of supper and a visit to a student production of the musical "Once upon a Mattress". The opening tableau of this stage spectacular depicted paunchy young men and ugly girls tripping haphazardly around the stage in flimsy night-dresses and bathing briefs to the hideous accompaniment of squeaky violins. This modest scene conjured up for Jonathan's partner visions of a potentially debauched and sinful theatrical evening. "I can't stand this frightful immorality," she said in a corncrake whisper. In fact, her fears were unjustified. Those who saw the show to the bitter end said that nothing took place upon the mattress even once.

Jonathan, who although he could have stood the so-called immorality, certainly could not stand the frightful orchestra, was happy to pander to his blind date's delicate susceptibilities and so led her away for a quick cup of coffee and early termination of his duties as an escort.

Michael, who had drawn even more unfavourably from the St Dunstan's lottery, was forced to sit through the play and go on to a party afterwards where he quickly found more alluring female companionship. The problem of how to dispose of the encumbrance of his blind date was solved by his charitable host, who trotted the poor girl off for a waltz.

Campus dances have an unwritten rule that any male spectator can, after a decent interval, tap a dancing male on the shoulder and steal his girl. This is known as "cutting in", a ruthless version of the English "excuse me" dance. The gallant host who had taken on Michael's date wished to be excused of her at the earliest opportunity. To speed this process he removed from his pocket a dollar bill which he waved provocatively behind the girl's back. Naturally there were plenty of impecunious takers and so from that moment on the girl had an even better evening than she would have had in the arms of a co-operative Beloff.

Ohio was indeed a happy hunting ground for amateur sexologists. After Denison we visited Hiram College (we reckoned it should have been called Harem), which is an establishment with a large surplus of predatory female students.

Our first day in the college we settled in for a comparatively early night, only to be aroused by frenzied tapping on the window-panes in the small hours. "Who's there?" There came the reply "Two young maids who just love your English accents." Though we suspected that this was not all that they loved, our gallantry and chivalry were aroused. We admitted our nocturnal visitors, only to find they were two specimens typecast to play the witches in Macbeth. One had a skin infection and yellow, dripping teeth; the other weighed fourteen stone and had not taken a bath for several weeks

The invaders treated us to a prolonged description of the sex life of the college which raised our eyebrows if not our hair. The witches indicated that they were normally enthusiastic participants in campus orgies but that they had been having a very dull time lately. They added, "Do you realize we could be expelled for this? Make it worth our while." Quickly pleading ill-health, fatigue, impotence and disease we managed to dismiss these vultures from our room with a reasonable amount of courtesy. We had no wish to rewrite our old school motto as "Defloreat Etona". It had been a narrow escape.

We spent another interesting weekend at the University of Wisconsin at Madison whose campus is dominated by a massive statue of a seated Abraham Lincoln. During our visit we were told by at least forty people about the university legend that Lincoln stands up and bows whenever a virgin passes his statue. Needless to say, he did not perform this ceremony during that weekend and it was good to have this confirmation that the great man's judgment was so sound.

Madison (which gave its name to the dance) is known as a "party school". Since we were invited to fourteen

102

parties in three days we thought the nickname well deserved. Alcohol is permitted on this particular campus; and inhibition was cast away with prohibition.

We stayed in an apartment which was shared by four students. Occassionally they stayed in it too. That weekend was not one of those occasions. Most of the time, as far as we could gather from their slurred and euphoric accounts, was spent by the shores of the nearby lake in moonlight clinches.

During those three days we had as many dates as a five-year calendar. The highspot was a ceremony known as a "hayride". This consists of a nocturnal trip in tractor-towed farm carts filled with prickly straw, and is fraught with sexual significance. The purpose of a "hayride" is to have a roll in the hay (known in Hollywood circles as "Splendour in the Grass"). All you need is a flask of brandy or bourbon and a willing girl.

After we had taken a car out to a local farm, we had to wait awhile for our more primitive carriages. Apparently the transport system is worked on a basis of free enterprise; and the highly sexed occupants of other nearby homes of learning had pre-empted the carts for the earlier part of the evening. Finally they arrived and we boarded them with a rush, clambering for the first-class seats by the side. The needle-like straw would have deterred an amorous fakir from denuding himself in preparation for a love bout; and the cold was such that only an Eskimo couple could possibly have braved the slightest exposure. The night air stillness was shattered by young American voices in full throat. Each traveller was called upon to contribute "The Yellow Rose of Texas", "Hello Lyndon", "Can't Buy me Love" and many another merry folk tune.

Some of the more exclusive confined themselves to self-adulatory fraternity and sorority chants.

> She may weigh two hundred and eighty-three
> But she's the only girl for me
> I'll forget she's got a nose like a hammer
> Because she is a Delta Gamma
>
> Her bust is huge and her brain is small
> But, jeez, that don't bug me at all
> She can't spell a word, and she don't know no grammar
> But she is still my Delta Gamma!

or words to that effect.

When it came to our turn we decided to pick on a duet version of the Eton Boating Song, which is in fact the only song of which we know both the tune and the words. Our musically proclaimed fondness for the open-air sport of rowing and our self-directed exhortations to "Swing, swing together with our bodies between our knees" evidently appalled our female companions who sought other solace in the straw. Clearly they would have preferred us to swing, swing together with their bodies between our knees. By such methods we once again escaped the clutches of the aggressive American female.

Another weird American sexual custom which we observed was the "pantie raid". We had the doubtful privilege of being spectators of two such raids, both instigated by girls.

The first was at Bucknell University in Pennsylvania. We were staying at an all-male fraternity house, and at dinner the student President announced "Y'all know the Theta Omega gals (a sorority, not a watch factory) are gonna try one of their pantie raids tonight. Be ready for 'em."

This announcement was greeted with much fruity chuckling, smacking of lips and thumping of tables. This beefy bunch of brothers evidently had no fear of losing their underwear.

The secret of all successful raids is to catch the enemy unawares and thus achieve victory. This military principle is reversed when it comes to pantie raids by college girls. Their object is defeat. They raid in order to lose their own pants. All publicity is therefore good publicity.

At the hour of midnight the fraternity house became aware of a shrill humming sound rapidly getting closer, as though a swarm of angry castrated bees was advancing. We peered anxiously from our window, at this time unversed in the conventions of clothes-warfare, and nervously tightened our pyjama cords. About thirty girls were sprinting towards the building; as they crossed the portals of the fraternity house, the vigilant brethren perched upon the roof-tops emptied several buckets of water upon the invaders. Shrieks rent the air. But water was not going to quench the indomitable Amazons' desire for pants losing. They entered the fraternity house which for the next ten minutes rocked upon its foundations. Then ominous silence. Finally the dishevelled maidens emerged from various doors, windows, hedgerows and parked automobiles in or near the house. The trickled off into the night, tittering happily at what had been truly satisfying defeat.

Our second pantie raid took place in Kentucky. On this occasion we were sitting in the common room of a men's dormitory discussing the great issues of the modern world in what is known as a bull session (an all male get-together). Our conversation was disturbed by the young ladies of an adjacent dormitory who evidently felt that bulls had others functions beside talking. These sirens were leaning out of their windows dangling negligées, brassières, underpants and other unmentionable articles, and were chanting a song whose opening words were:

> We don't wear bras and we don't wear pants
> We like to give the freshmen a chance
> Why don't you come up and start a romance
> We're the girls from campus hall.

This musical masterpiece was accompanied by glass-breaking falsetto yells of "Yip! Yip! Yip! Come and get it! Yip! Yip!"

The members of the bull session sprang to action. First they mustered recruits by hammering on the doors of somnolent freshmen. "Say, do you know what the girls from Rubinstein Dorm have been saying about ya?" On hearing the ladies' message the slighted freshmen rose to the challenge. Soon we had fifty young males, blood coursing through their veins, chomping and stamping in the hall.

At the inspiring command of "OK boys!" the charge commenced. Evelyn Waugh in *Decline and Fall* describes an Oxford riot dominated by "The sound of English county families baying for broken glass". It is a sound still heard occasionally in Oxford of the 1960s, but as war-cries go it pales into insignificance when compared to the sound of Midwestern college students baying for sex.

As the attacking battalion advanced with a slow loping stride much time was spent slapping one's own thighs and one's neighbour's buttocks with unrestrained heartiness.

106

In our midst were two or three individuals with musical
instruments. A guitar, a trumpet, a mouth organ and a
kazzooka (a comb wrapped in lavatory paper through
which one emitted a refined hum), all made themselves
heard noisily and frequently. Everyone was shouting at
the top of their voices. "Yoop a de Yoop a de Yoop! Ouch!
Ow! Grrup! Grrupp! Rah! Rah! Rah!" were the most
audible group noises, but there were many fine individual
contributions such as:

"Betcha Bill's first inside Betsy Busker!"

"Six pairs o' cami knickers'll look good on my wall."

"Yoicks, Yoicks, give 'em de woicks!"

We entered the Rubinstein dorm en masse, only to find
that the vast majority of girls had thought better of their
offer and had retreated behind double-locked doors in the
washroom. About half-a-dozen of the underwear-dangling
playmates had dallied in their cubicles, however, and these
were duly deprived of their pants. (Or so we assumed. Since
twelve burly freshmen operated on each girl it was impossible to see what was going on.)

After these executions, frustration set in amongst the
invading party. They had not had enough to do.

"Let's have Al's pants," someone yelled. Al was de-
bagged. Then it was Seth's turn, then Dwight's, then
Morgan's . . . an all-male orgy was in process. We left it
hurriedly when we heard the chief debater whom we had
vanquished earlier in the day mutter huskily, "Where are
those guys from England?"

Our experience of the totem and taboo of the American
student tribes had left us a little bewildered. It was clear
at any rate that the sexual mores were not the legacy of the
earliest invaders like the Pilgrim Fathers. Maybe, of course,

they date back to the indigenous Red Indians. Apart from a few natural beauties we thought that the campus womenhood lacked style, grace and sophistication—and we wish to put it on record that Bermuda shorts far outrank Fidel Castro as the biggest Caribbean menace to the American way of life. They are definitely not the last word in elegance, when drawn taut across the buttocks fattened on a diet of french fries and gluttinous chocolate shakes. But what she lacks in style, the American maiden makes up for in enthusiasm. On most campuses there is certainly no shyness of the male sex. Co-education has worked away that particular sin. And we wonder in how many English universities it would be possible to find so many "blind dates" for visitors from abroad—not all of whom by any means were frustrated or frigid wallflowers!

Indeed American campus' sexual custom is an odd mixture of elaborate ritual and free and easy practice. Though everywhere students seemed to find inexplicable the English notion that one could have six different dates in six nights—none of whom need be serious passions, none of whom would demand loyalty oaths—the institution of the blind date shows that not all relationships run on the railways of convention. Apparently it is all right to be "promiscuous" (we use the word in a non-technical sense) as long as you don't actually *choose* your partners in advance.

Alas, the attitudes of the College authorities seem to be as primitive as their English counterparts. Co-education is accepted, but controlled. In Wooster College, Ohio (admittedly no standard example, as it was a strongly religious institution), the twist had been banned until very recently on the ground that it was an incitement to concupiscence. Here our student chauffeur informed us with great pride that he had taken his girl friend to have a roll in his flat before coming out to meet us. It turned out that this was not a sexual revelation, but a gastronomic one. The punchline came with the information that he risked a fine of a hundred dollars for so doing! The rules as regards "having men (or women) in your rooms" on American campuses make Oxford look like a Wayland Young Utopia. For when residential quarters are barred as rendezvous the result is inevitable. Michael gave vent to some pompous utterances for the *Daily Illini*. "He thought it rather strange," the journalist reported, "that men and women students are not permitted in one another's dorms. They are thereby forced to make an obvious and discourteous display of affection in lounges which in England can be kept more in private". Indeed, the age of public love was upon us. And the chaste and the scholarly can hardly get back to their rooms at night from long hours in the library, as every available entrance is blocked by entwined bodies. Some entrepreneur should establish kissing meters to ease the problem.

At Bates College, Maine, attempts were being made to achieve a breakthrough. There was a pioneer movement to allow men in women's dormitories on Sundays between midday and five in the afternoon. (They are banned during the week!) Unfortunately, we were told, a strong rearguard action was being fought by a group of bashful virgins, who were adamantly opposed to any intrusion on their privacy. Indeed, although Bates was one of the most attractive Liberal Arts Colleges that we visited, we found nothing very liberal about it as far as boy/girl relationships were concerned. Co-education had been extended from the classroom to the dining hall. But all that happened was

109

that the boys sat one end, the girls at the other, and the dating couples conspicuous in between.

At another East Coast college we found an example of where the Puritan wishes of the founder had been frustrated. The College authorities had had rooms built for the girls that were so small, with scarcely room for more than a bed, that male friends would be discouraged from paying visits. But as a result, those who did come could only do one thing when they got there.

At Madison, where, as we have indicated, a Polynesian Islander might find himself regarded as a square, the tide of progress has swept into the lobbies at the bottom of the residential blocks. Here dating couples can bid their fond adieus amid the chromium sofas. But authority remains in the persons of the house fellows, graduate girl students selected for their high calling on grounds of purity and unswerving devotion to established principles. These custodians of the public morality take the night-watch in turn. Their duty is to prevent friendliness from developing into intimacy. One sophomore shoe has but to leave the carpet, one sophomore leg to lie upon the couch, and the house fellow is at hand to re-set the couple in less dangerous positions. The whole procedure is highly entertaining, as these hen-like prefects scuttle from a first sighing duo to a second, their success in one corner inevitably balanced out by their failure in another.

But, whatever may be the attitudes of authority, we would hesitate to say that the colleges are acting as trustees for the parents. After all, the middle-class parents' antidote to modern morals is to accelerate modern marriage. In this perhaps their judgment is questionable. "For they that sow in fraternity pins shall reap in alimony" (saith the prophet Jonathan).

7

Fraternities and Other Tribal Rites

AMERICA is the land of liberty, equality and fraternities. The first two flourish despite, not because of, the last. If we wanted to spark off a controversial passionate discussion among students on almost any campus we would start asking questions not about the race issue, nor about Johnson and Goldwater, nor about Vietnam. Instead, we would innocently enquire about the merits and de-merits of the fraternity system.

The whole concept of fraternities seems weird to English eyes. Imagine one of the new English universities stocked with good residential accommodation for both male and female students, and equipped with fine facilities in reading rooms, television lounges, recreation halls and libraries. This would be the university of milk and honey—hard to think of further improvements.

One finds such facilities on most American campuses. The welfare, leisure and habitation of the student population is lavishly catered for, but in America a feast is never enough. Fraternities are born of the occupational malady of transatlantic life—craving for status. All students are equal, but some want to be more equal than others and these form themselves into residential clubs which only the acceptable are invited to join. Fraternity brethren spurn the palatial domestic edifices erected by the university and build for themselves near the campus large sprawling houses which, though inferior in comfort and convenience, are superior in social status. Forty or so like-minded men, or if it is a sorority, women, form themselves into self-electing élites and live, often in conditions of overcrowded squalor, in these separate houses.

We found on arriving on a campus that there is something almost sinister about the stranglehold which the fraternity system has on so many universities. We would be led on to the centre of the campus; we would have shown to us the magnificent modern architecture of the campus library, the administration building, the chapel, the science laboratories and the new dormitories, but then our hosts would point to a scraggy line of gloomy-looking houses (with strange Greek symbols painted above their porches) just off the central area. As we lifted up our eyes unto the fraternity houses, our hosts would speak of them sometimes in reverential tones of pride and enthusiasm, sometimes in tones of hope, sometimes in tones of contempt and disgust, depending on whether the student to whom we were talking was a member, might be a member, or had refused to become or been refused becoming a member of one of the fraternities.

We were then, if our host was a brother of a fraternity, often taken to dinner in his house. We would be shown into a dining hall containing about fifty young men, all standing respectfully until the guests of honour arrived and grace was said. The meal would be frequently worse, and rarely better, than the food in the campus cafeteria. After the meal there would be a short period of announcements, which invariably included a request (always granted) for a round of applause for our guests from Britain—in Sigma Chi they snap their fingers rather than clap their hands—an announcement about a forthcoming sporting fixture from netball to a pantie raid, and sometimes a complaint or two to the effect that some unknown brothers had been removing iced beer from the refrigerator without paying for it.

After this we would be shown over the fraternity house. What struck us most was the indescribable squalor in which most bands of brothers chose to live. A fraternity house is a strictly functional building. On the ground floor there is usually a large room in which the brothers can permanently loiter and discuss their girls, their athletic achievements and their politics, so that everyone else can hear. Usually in the hall there is a notice-board whose notices range from announcements of religious services to one jewel found in Denison, Ohio, which contained a list of names headed by the words, "The following guys are being dominated by their women. They have gone out at least three times and nothing has happened (!!!)." Off the entrance hall there is the dining room and behind that the kitchen, and also somewhere close to the entrance hall there is a small room euphemistically known as the reading room. It contains large leatherbound volumes coated in dust, its walls are hung with photographs of former brothers of the fraternity interspersed with stags' heads, and the benches are strewn with dog-eared copies of colour comics (a sample title "Superman Marvel and the Sin Lovers") and old copies of *Playboy* with many pages cut out. In the basement, which serves the dual purpose of fall-out shelter and necking room, is the television set. This was the

113

most highly populated room in any fraternity house and was invariably in total darkness. About fifteen brothers sat hunched intently around a vast screen watching the inevitable football game or Western. In other unlit corners of the room could be found beer drinkers (illegal according to the strict rules of the campus) and sometimes we stumbled over bundles on the floor which, on closer inspection, turned out to be a brother and sister (in the fraternity rather than the family sense of the word) from a nearby sorority playing "smacky mouth" (American name for smooching, snogging, etc). Upstairs there are a number of tiny little studies, although only the name denoted an atmosphere of learning and industry. These studies were ten foot by eight and were shared by five or six brothers. Half the room was invariably taken up by an enormous hi-fi set which blared incessantly and six cases of records. The walls were plastered with "Playmates of the Month"— nude centre-spread colour photographs ripped from the pages of *Playboy* we had seen in the reading room. There was one chair usually submerged by records and in order to get into the room one had to march across a sea of soiled underwear. On the floor above the studies there would be a vast dormitory which consisted of about thirty beds standing on the floor and another twenty beds standing on racks above the first layer of beds. None of the beds seemed to have been made for at least six weeks, the stench was overpowering and the whole scene resembled a sort of mass extension of an insalubrious couchette on a French train.

The most pertinent comment on the lowering of standards that one undergoes in a fraternity is revealed in the following story. One night in Illinois we were offered a guest room with only one bed, and made a jocular protest about this to our hosts. Some months later an American visitor to Oxford, on being introduced by chance to Michael, said, "Why, aren't you the guy who made that remark about the bed out in Illinois State?" He was, of course, from a different campus. Our little stand for comfort had become a Midwestern fraternity talking point. Like Oliver Twist we had dared to ask for more.

We found it difficult to understand why any students should wish to change the neat individual accommodation usually provided in campus dormitories for the life of mass uncleanliness and ungodliness offered by fraternities. But when we voiced our incomprehension amongst the brethren we were automatically met by a flood of slogans, possibly learnt by heart, in defence of the system. "Fraternities give us a real sense of being members of a community. . . . We put the house before ourselves. . . . We're predominantly altruistic organisations. . . . We contribute to the spirit of the university. . . . We make deeper friendships here than you would in dormitories." One student, from Bucknell University, we remember especially for the piety of his short homily. He described how he had come up to the university, a cocky high-school kid, king of the football field, and how he had learnt through his fraternity life the virtues of corporate spirit and character building. It was odd to hear the sentiments of the English public school headmaster coming from the mouth of this vital crew-cut young American.

From the opponents of the system we got a different picture. "Fraternities are places which charge a thousand dollars a year for letting you choose your own friends. . . . Yeah, they're communities all right but they're communities built on snobbery and self-interest. . . . They are just a beery camaraderie of guys with plenty of money and no interest in study. . . . They are so altruistic that three national fraternities have clauses in their oaths of admission which make it impossible for Negroes and non-Christians to join. . . . When they talk of contributing spirit I guess they are referring to all that smuggled liquor, and deeper friendships mean basement orgies. . . . No sensitive person could possibly stand fraternity life."

We met indeed many who had only joined through a sense of loyalty to their parents, and who found themselves hard pressed to justify their attachment on any rational grounds. "The Greeks" is the cynical name given to fraternity members by those left outside in the warm. This refers to their alphabetical title rather than to any causal connection with the pioneers of Western civilisation.

We kept completely open minds on the issue until we reached the grass roots of the fraternity system deep in the Midwest. There we got a comprehensive introduction to the pledge system. Pledges are students in their first or second year who are asked to join fraternities on a probationary basis. Although they can use the facilities of the fraternity house to some extent, they do not become full members until they have been initiated and they are not initiated until they have served about a nine month period of training designed to test their mettle to the full. (In sororities the grosser excesses of apprenticeship are spared the girls, and they have instead to wear placards around their necks for extended periods rather like prize entries at Crufts.)

The first time we encountered the pledging system occurred when we were walking across the campus in

116

Pennsylvania with a senior student who had, up to that point, seemed a model of sensible maturity. In the middle of being shown around by him he suddenly broke into a frenzied sprint away from us and dived behind a nearby pillar. A few seconds later a younger student carrying a grubby notebook puffed into view and enquired of us, "Say, where's Ikey Finberger gone?" Perceiving from our departed friend's behaviour that this innocent-looking questioner was evidently a dangerous enemy, we sent him off in a false direction. When our friend reappeared he explained his sudden bolt for hiding, "That guy's one of the pledges from my fraternity. He's on an initiative test and every day for a week he has to collect the signatures of all fifty of the brothers in our fraternity, but I sure fooled him today."

In Whitewater, Wisconsin, we descended on the campus during "Hell Week". This was too polite a term for it in our opinion since all the pledges from all the fraternities were going through a strenuous seven days of every conceivable form of so-called initiative test. Thus when we went into the university cafeteria we were introduced to several girls whose response to our British "How do you do's" was merely to giggle excitedly and shake and nod their heads like donkeys. Full of the courtesies of civilisation we endeavoured to make polite conversation with these figures. "What are you studying?" "Are you coming to our debate?" "Did you watch the football team last Saturday?" All our small talk was met with silence. Our hosts also fired questions at these unfortunate mutes. Finally, their urge to hear more of the beautiful British accent broke down their silence and they talked to us. At this there were yells of delight from our hosts. The girls, in order to win

117

admission to their sororities, had taken an oath of silence not to speak to any man for seven days. Their lapse into conversation was no aspersion on our virility. We had caused them to break their trappist vows and as a result their admission to fraternities would be delayed for yet another week.

But it was at Denison, Ohio, that we came across the pièce de résistance of pledging absurdity. The pledges in the Sigma Chi Fraternity House were evidently an obstreperous bunch, for they were greatly addicted to the practice of playing practical so-called jokes upon their lords and masters, the regular faternity brethren. During our visit, while the senior fraternity brethren were slumbering in their fifty bed attic in the fraternity house, the fun-loving pledges acquired a large tin of automobile grease which they dexterously smeared all over the top floor of the fraternity house, especially in the area between the beds and bathroom. Thus when the high and mighty rose to perform their morning ablutions they slithered in hopelessly undignified postures around through the sea of auto-grease. This was a crime of great magnitude and the head of the fraternity planned fitting retaliation against his pledges.

One of the duties of the senior brethren is apparently to make sure that the pledges are kept in a fine state of physical fitness. This is achieved by work-outs or physical training sessions which are compulsory for all pledges (compulsory only if you suffer from the misguided motive to wish to become a member of a fraternity in the first place). It was thus planned that a work-out should be held as one brother put it, "To knock the spunk out of those doggone grease merchants." We were invited to watch the spectacle of the work-out. One of the brothers had served for two years in the Marines before coming to university. This, he proudly informed us, had taught him to regard all human physical weaknesses with complete contempt, and he had also acquired a rich vocabulary of four-letter words without which no military discipline could, in his opinion, be satisfactorily achieved. The pledges, numbering about fifteen, were lined up and treated to a brusque speech, the essential message of which was (in acceptable vernacular) "You're a lousy lot of bums." This oration lasted approximately twelve minutes and the ex-Marine displayed to the full his versatility with bad language as he did not repeat any one swear word during this address. After this his tone changed to a benign and rather chummy "Come on, fellahs, let's co-operate" tone, and he politely requested the pledges to move the six heavy oak tables and fifty chairs from the dining room on the ground floor into the basement. This laborious and exhausting task was achieved, whereupon the pledges were promptly ordered to move them back again. As soon as they had moved them back to the dining room they were told that they had fulfilled the task in a surly manner which disgraced the good name of the fraternity, so would they please show a bit more community spirit and move all that furniture back to the basement again. When it was in the basement they were then informed that they had taken an absurdly long time fulfilling a very simple manoeuvre and they had darn well better improve on their timing during the next couple of shifts. We witnessed this dining room to basement and back again cycle no less than six times, at the end of which two chairs had been broken, considerable damage had been done to the structure and décor of the fraternity house, and

119

one of the pledges claimed to have fractured a toe. This made no impact on the sadistic ex-Marine who briskly observed, "Now the work-out is gonna start".

The perspiring pledges, who thought it had already finished, looked distressed, but they were lined up in the entrance hall and put through an astonishing series of exhausting physical jerks. Each pledge was supervised by three senior brethren who at the slightest sign of fatigue from their victim would give him a hearty kick or wallop with the nearest offensive weapon. When the tender-hearted Jonathan indulged in a tactful criticism of this procedure to the vice-president of the fraternity, he was told that this was a normal tradition of hazing which had, in fact, been bowdlerised for the benefit of their English visitors. "We all had to go through it, and they all enjoy it anyway," he assured us, with all the serious conviction of an English master of foxhounds informing critics the fox enjoys being hunted. "But now we'll show you something with the heat really on," he grinned. Those of the pledges who were still alive were ordered to strip down to their underpants and to bend down, putting their index fingers on to a chalk-marked spot on the floor. They were then commanded to run round in a small tight circle always keeping their fingers pressed to the spot. In order to ensure that the pledges did not try and modify this exhausting torture by running round at a slow pace, the brethren lit up fat cigars, not for smoking purposes, but in order that the singeing ends might be applied to any posterior which was revolving at an inadequate speed. The unfortunate pledges had thus to choose between a stomach-turning feat of high-speed acrobatics or a singed behind and, of course, most of them got the worst of both worlds. The

120

exercise terminated only when either the cigars had gone out or when the pledges collapsed, some vomiting, some screaming, and some unconscious with dizziness, on the floor. It was a viciously unpleasant scene and it left a nasty taste in the mouth. .

But the extraordinary thing about this is that it is completely voluntary. Everyone knows that this sort of thing does go on in certain fraternity houses. No one becomes a pledge to a fraternity unless he has a positive wish to do so. Moreover, as both pledges and brethren told us, it is a well-known fraternity tradition that if pledges play practical jokes on the brothers the brothers retaliate with this sort of work-out session. This was emphasised by the fact that the morning after the scene which had horrified us, all the brothers woke up to find that the pledges had overnight placed glue in their shoes and, of course, the glue meant another work-out session that evening. Thus we were left with the inescapable conclusion that what we would call horrifying sadism goes on because the people concerned positively wish it to continue. The same is true for not only the physical endurance tests but also for the more nonsensical traditions.

Of course, not all fraternity ceremonies display cruelty. Sometimes they merely display crudity. Our ex-Marine buddy described to us the festivities of Derby day at the Sigma Chis. This holiday is not connected with horses, but with horsing around. Girls from sororities pursue men with hats (derbies) bent on snatching them away; and apparently during the rough-and-tumble many a clean limbed American boy has his clean limbs exposed. Afterwards there are milking contests and other still more bucolic activities. The crowning moment comes when three

121

"experienced" males are tied to a tree, and three "experienced" girls undulate up against them. The scene would grace the memoirs of a Christian anchorite in the later Roman Empire.

We gradually got used to all the various external aspects of fraternity life. The secret handshakes which, when demonstrated to the novices from Britain, left us wringing crippled arthritic fingers for weeks afterwards; the corny in-jokes between brothers; the comic figures known as house-mothers who are jolly middle-aged matrons (like Dames at Eton) appointed by certain richer fraternities to supervise the domestic trivia of each local chapter; and all the absurdities of hell-weeks, and pledging.

What we never got used to was the status-consciousness of fraternities. America is often described as a classless society. Superficially it certainly seems to be more of one than Britain, but whereas in Britain the Establishment remains powerful by inviting anyone of obvious talent, whatever his origins, to join it, in America the Establishment flourishes by rigorously excluding anyone who does not measure up to the most exacting standards of acceptability. American élites are built on the blackball system, and nowhere is this more true than in fraternities.

After listening to countless discussions between faternity brothers as to which of this year's freshmen should be "rushed" (asked to join the house), it was plain to us that the qualifications for becoming a fraternity brother are often more negative than positive. "He wouldn't fit" is the most pejorative comment that can be made about a potential candidate. The reasons for not fitting were many and varied. Ugliness is one. Several of the students we debated against claimed to have been excluded from fraternities because their political views were too liberal. Negroes never stand a hope of getting elected, except in one or two remarkable local chapters where a revolution has been fought and won for their admission. The fact that new members must be felt to be acceptable to old ones means that the contemporary admissions system is governed by the prejudices of the past. The religious content of initiation oaths bar Jewish students, but with typical resourcefulness they have founded their own exclusively Jewish fraternities. The fraternities at Columbia, for example, are split religiously 50–50 into Christian houses and Jewish houses. Wealth, car ownership and social backgrounds all count significantly in determining the suitability of a candidate. None of the smart clubs at Oxford or Cambridge, such as the Pitt or the Gridiron, would ever dare to stoop to the cold-blooded social scrutiny that is common in fraternity elections.

One evening we witnessed a strange ceremony which emphasised the whole self-perpetuating snobbery of fraternities.

At Hiram College, Ohio, we were returning stealthily to our sleeping quarters (trying to avoid the predatory female vultures described earlier) when we observed an immaculately formed semi-circle of white-robed figures standing around the porch of a fraternity house.

The semi-circle consisted of twenty maidens clad in long white dresses similar to the absurd costumes worn by London debutantes when they go through the cocoon stage of becoming social butterflies at Queen Charlotte's Ball. The men were in white flannel suits, their faces shining with Max Factor after-shave lotion, a complete transformation from their ultra-informal garb of jeans and tee

123

shirts which is the normal academic dress of most campuses.

All heads seemed to be bowed in prayer. One of the young men leant forward and lit a tiny bonfire in the middle of the semi-circle. Then, at a nod from him, the entire group broke reverently and solemnly into what they evidently considered was a sonorous and moving melody.

What could this be? A meeting of a branch of the Ku Klux Klan? A religious ceremony for young American Druids? Or the procuring of vestal virgins before the slaughter?

While these thoughts were passing through our minds, behold the doors of the fraternity house opened and an even more immaculate young man and woman stepped forth into the middle of the semi-circle which ceased singing, bowed respectfully to these Klan Chiefs or High Priests and then burst into song once again. Five or six songs were performed, each one more solemn and holy than the last. Perhaps someone had died recently and this was a sort of musical memorial service?

Finally the music stopped. "Three cheers for Homer and Blossom," shouted someone. At this everyone clapped loudly and the semi-circle of acolytes broke up into an orgy of handshaking accompanied by shouts of goodwill such as "And breed lots of Theta Epsilon Kappa babies".

We stood scratching our heads still none the wiser. On enquiry we discovered that this ceremony is held every time a boy from the Theta Epsilon Kappa gets pinned to a girl from the Theta Epsilon Kappa sorority. Plans had been made for the cream of society to marry the cream of society and great is the rejoicing thereof. One happy result is that their children will undoubtedly in their day become Theta Epsilon Kappas also and so on ad infinitum. Even the French aristocracy before the revolution could

124

not have excelled this type of matrimonial introspection.

Fraternities give the lie to the notion that America is a country concerned only with the future, and heedless of the numbing grasp of the past, careless of tradition, sceptical of the irrational. Where the clubs of Oxbridge perpetuate a class structure, the fraternities of the New World create one. They are incubators for immaturity. They perpetuate in their members all the silliness of adolescence just at a time when students ought to be awakening to the excitements and responsibilities of university life. They foster the most absurd and archaic traits of the English public school, and they foster them among people already well past the age of schoolboys. The cruelty and stupidity of the initiation ceremonies recall the tales told in the autobiographies of nineteenth-century old Etonians, who never grew up. The duties of pledge apprenticeship are a direct American imitation of the fagging system. The compulsive gamesiness of public school life is reborn once again. Fraternities fossilise a teenage attitude to women in twenty-year-olds. The value of personal relationships is scarcely considered. The spirit of the chase, of treating women as prey to be overcome, is intensified in the crude and boastful barrack-room atmosphere. And who should be surprised when in fraternities the ideal is not the potential wife, the girl-next-door writ large, but rather the exotic fantasy of the "girly magazine", the Playmate of the Midwestern world? Fraternities emphasise a synthetic community spirit, often in highly frivolous form—but they breed intolerance of minorities, a blind desire to conform to a pattern of unswerving normality. The "good chap" of the Old World becomes the "swell guy" of the New. And who worries about those who suffer exclusion?

125

Fraternities do their utmost to distract their members from deeper academic study. In most houses the brother who would prefer to spend his Saturday afternoon reading Gibbon and Macaulay to sitting in front of the TV set watching the ball game would be jeered, not cheered. "He wouldn't fit," the brethren would say of such an individual when his name comes up for rushing. No wonder the teachers on all campuses were, almost to a man, hostile to the whole system.

But although we believe our opinions to be true today, the most encouraging aspect of fraternities is that their grip on university campuses is steadily weakening. Numerically they are still powerful. At Columbia thirty per cent of all students belong to a fraternity. At Whitewater, Wisconsin, the figure is about eighty per cent, and most campuses are somewhere between these figures.

Yet so many university students and faculty members hold the view that fraternities are opposed to everything a good university stands for, that fraternity prestige is at a low ebb. At famous Williamsburg, Mass., fraternities have been abolished entirely. At Florida Presbyterian College, a university started in 1960, fraternities were never allowed to start. At Wabash College, Indiana, several leading undergraduates had resigned from their chapters in protest against discrimination clauses in fraternity oaths of admission. Everywhere there is strong anti-fraternity criticism.

These are encouraging signs, but meanwhile we should remember the way in which fraternities span the nation. In them are created almost Masonic loyalties. Presidents of the houses still meet at congresses like teenage Trade Union leaders. The old boys will fight on. The Bourbons have not lost the battle yet.

8

Race '64

IT'S HARD for the traveller in America to say or think anything new about what they call the colour problem. His interest has something in it of the voyeur's. It is a trifle over-enthusiastic, a trifle indecent. We feel perhaps a sense of shame when we remember the growing anticipation with which we awaited our descent into the South. There we would be in the heart of it all, knights in our liberal armour, who would escape to tell with ever so slight an air of superiority our first-hand impressions of America's reincarnated civil war.

And yet not to say anything would be false and stupid. Re-reading a travel book about America written in the aftermath of the second World War, one is struck by the casual and slightly curious way in which the Negro question is touched upon. It's hard to remember that but fifteen years ago the subordination of this large ethnic minority group was taken for granted. The visitor noticed indeed; he criticised perforce; but really his attitude was like that of the sophisticated history schoolsman who knows that it is a little naïve to apply the moral standards of one's own country and age to that of another society. But in 1964 one couldn't be detached. Everywhere the dialogue continued.

We wanted to talk and they wanted to talk. Like strangers introduced at a party we could seize upon this theme as something to break down the conventional barriers of reserve. What we heard, what we said, was merely the echo of thousands of other conversations, transmitted by print and screen across the Atlantic. There was always the sense of *déjà entendu*, if never of *déjà vu*. But if it wasn't easy to believe or understand, it was impossible to forget.

We remember that from the very first day in New York what struck us so forcibly was that the Plimsoll line of society was demarcated in black and white. Your road-sweepers, your hotel porters, your waiters, your domestic staff were black. And above this stretched the white hierarchy. Those Negroes we met on the campuses with ambition to turn their education to profit in their careers were emphatic on the disability of the colour of their skin. To be a Negro lawyer or a Negro doctor one has, it seems, to cater for a clientèle of one's own race. There weren't that many opportunities to speak to Negro students. And anyhow, how do you speak to a "problem"? On November 3rd —Polling Day in the Presidential election—Michael was driven by a twenty-two-year-old Negro student who was going into Cleveland to exercise a right given to him by law and geographical circumstances.

"It's LBJ for me," he said. "It's not that I've got anything personal against Goldwater. . . . "

Michael asked him about himself.

"My parents came from Mississippi and they moved up north just as soon as they could afford to get out. Sometimes I'm not certain how good a thing it is. There's better money. We've been able to move out into the suburbs above the city. But as far as being a Negro's concerned, I'm not sure

128

that there's much to choose between Southern honesty and Northern hypocrisy. There's not one of my friends who isn't deeply involved in what's happening now. I don't think whites realize that we're not just a problem that they're going to solve in their own time. The summer riots may have disturbed a lot of whites. But they made a whole lot more sit up and take notice. This is the number one problem of this country. I just want to be an American like everyone else. As it is, I'm a Negro first and an American second. You just can't escape your colour. At a small college like Hiram mixed dating's virtually impossible. The pressures on the white girl are too great. Everyone notices, everyone talks—and the parents hate it. Why is it all Americans think that integration is the first step to mass mixed marriages? Anyone would imagine that the Negro has some weird power to compel a white girl to marry him. Love should be a personal matter."

"What about the Black Muslims?"

"They've got much more appeal than people imagine. I don't agree with their views on separatism. But at least they give a man a pride in his blackness. Why is it that the word 'black' always means something bad in Western vocabulary?"

"And what do you think will happen in the end?"

"Oh, it'll all work out for the best. But maybe I'm just an optimist about human nature."

Perhaps he was, for the history of the street where he lived was a very savage comment on the American future. Segregation and poverty one accepts as normal allies; segregation and affluence is harder to comprehend. And yet here we were in a leafy suburb, high above the heat of the city; wide, spacious streets. This was no slumland, and

129

yet there was not a white face in sight. All down the lawns that fringed the road, like obscene kinds of tree, For Sale notices tokened the last wave of the white emigration. It evidently isn't enough for a Negro to establish himself as economically middle class to be accepted as a neighbour by his white fellow-countrymen. The sad drama of apartheid is simply played out at the six thousand dollar level. A black Hampstead.

Lower down the echelons of society it was easier to see. "If you really go into Harlem, just 'phone us if you get out," the head of the British Information Service said to us. It wasn't really a joke. Americans were apt to lose their tempers when we said that it was somewhat discreditable that one couldn't walk the streets of their major cities safely. At this stage cutlery would be banged, and remarks about "offshore islands" and a "nation of beefeaters" would volley forth.

Harlem, South Side Chicago, the rotten core of the big industrial cities, where only the poorest still live—the pattern repeats itself across the north. Most vivid for us was the day on which we took a car through Philadelphia, and penetrated layer by layer the body of the fourth largest conurbation in America. It took us half-an-hour to cross the Negro ghetto, scene of the bitter flare of the summer riots. Blood coloured slums lowered across narrow streets, the rusty fire escapes like vines on their sides. An air of extreme poverty and ugliness, cracked paintwork, broken and boarded windows, the scars of the July violence. Dusk was closing in. Already the knots of gangs tightened on the corners. The prostitutes crept from their apartments. Small Negro children with their relentless, sad expressions, muffled to the ears in windcheaters, kicked the inevitable

130

football along the pavement. We didn't see a white face anywhere. Indeed, it was only the extremely old and indigent whites who remained there faute de mieux. The main shopping streets, flashy with neon bulb, had a gayer, noisier style. But the Negro colony is there, a fixed immovable cancer in the body of the city, making a mockery of those who think that a few bills passed through Congress will erase the legacy of decades. Remembering our Cleveland experience, we asked our American friends what they thought that the Negro could do. An argument developed about the ethics of the middle-class Negro voyage to the suburbs. One said that those who moved into white suburbs were simply troublemakers. There were places that they could go unopposed, which had just as pleasant an environment. The idea of the community with its local prides and tender newborn traditions was carefully fostered by the whites. Why should their modus vivendi be disturbed? All this said with rational calm. He had no wish to deny Negroes equal rights; only, it seemed, equal rights in the same place. And he admitted that since he had been brought up in an all white neighbourhood he might himself be prejudiced.

Later, when we were at Hampton College in Norfolk, Virginia, the whole question was brought back to mind by a performance that we saw of Lorraine Hansberry's *Raisin in the Sun*. The play, about a Negro family in Chicago, focuses on their attempt to start a new life in a new house out in a prosperous suburb. And in one scene a white emissary comes to try to buy them out, using the arguments used by our friend in Philadelphia. Of all the college productions that we saw in America this was by far the best acted. But the experience of watching a play in an

131

audience to whom every line of the fiction is a reflection of their own experience is one that one undergoes very rarely. The audience were in their laughter and applause partisan as much as appreciative, willing the actors along to the triumphant conclusion that the play reaches.

This wasn't just a Southern issue. Odd fragments of information were collected for the scrapbag in almost every place to which we went. Where there wasn't a specific local colour problem, some question of housing, education, law and order, people would comment cheerfully on its absence. At Edinboro Teachers' Training College in Erie, Pennsylvania, the speech professor told us that there was only one Negro family in the whole town, and that what Negroes there were on campus were "carefully hand-picked". With an ironic bitterness he said how difficult it was to teach in those circumstances. "Fail a white student, and you're maintaining academic standards; fail a Negro, and you're exhibiting colour prejudice." One student from Virginia was against the Civil Rights Bill. His father owned a restaurant, and compulsory integration meant falling trade and falling profits. Again, like our friend from Philadelphia, there was no trace of a redneck unthinking racialism. Just another example of someone whose personal security was threatened in the movement towards emancipation. But there was passion from another faculty member on the need to obliterate "a hundred years of guilt".

Up in Wabash, Indiana, once a centre of the Ku Klux Klan, the wife of the debates coach said that when they entertained Negro students at home, neighbours would comment with surprise and criticism. And even in this Midwestern town a latent segregation persisted in bar and barber shop. The college was the only employer of white-

132

collar black staff. But as she said, one was caught in a cleft stick. You couldn't pretend to treat as absolutely ordinary people whom those around you treated as inferiors. "When a beer party looks like a kind of demonstration, what are you to do?" Everywhere there was the sign of this liberal dilemma. How do you tread the tightrope between intolerance and condescension? How do you fight a battle that you think should have been won many years before? Even we as outsiders would find ourselves trapped into posing artificial questions. "Why did you come here particularly?" Michael asked the white English teacher at Hampton College, Virginia, an all black school. "The money was better. We're not martyrs or missionaries, you know." But then what of the time in Normal, Illinois, when, in the course of an excellent dinner at an expensive restaurant, we were forced into a discussion of whether or not there had ever been slavery in England, while a coloured waiter listened and served impassively? These are the new embarrassments of this age. And being strangers we were more sensitive than most to the absurdities of these recurrent situations.

And so down South. Our sense of adventure had been matched in the words of the people we met up North. They at least were willing to imagine that we were crossing a vital boundary between one culture and another. Of course, this was another revelation of the way in which America's sheer size plays a part in its politics. Very few of those who made the jokes about lynchings and burning crosses had ever been south of the Mason Dixon line. They really were talking about a foreign country, as strange to them as it was to us.

And for all the importance that the Civil Rights movement has not only for the America of the 1960s but for the future of the democratic values of the West, few had gone down South to participate or even to find out. If one were to seek a likely analogy to the Civil Rights issue for contemporary England, one would seize upon CND. But one would be wrong. The question with its moral tinder had conspicuously failed to set alight, as far as we could see, the average college student.

Students may be the leaders of protest movements; overall there is little protest. Perhaps it was natural that Oxford, the home of lost causes, should by the law of averages find itself a hotbed of a movement like the Campaign for Nuclear Disarmament. Though the issue is buried for the moment, the initial impetus lost, the enthusiasm generated by it diverted into other channels, the memory remains of an Oxford of but five years back passionately divided into the two camps: those with badges and those without. Even the apolitical Christ Church "bloody" would play his clownish role in the great debate by seizing upon the CND student specifically rather than any old grammar school scientist in order to work off his Eights Week high spirits. But on an American campus, though the moral issue was so much more clearly defined, though this particular progressive sin was political orthodoxy at the highest level, we found little evidence that the movement had captured the imagination. Indeed, of the two conversations that we had with those who had gone down South to help in the project to register the freshly emancipated Negro voter, one was with an English student from Cambridge and now at Yale. Of the value of what had been done in the summer, he had no doubt. "They looked on us as something heaven sent; almost as messiahs. They couldn't believe that at last someone cared enough to come." Another, an American student at Wabash, told us more dramatically of threats of railroading and of anxious moments waiting for the return of a carload of racist bullies. One can say in extenuation of the American student that the dangers involved in the summer project in Mississippi (when, as is known the world over, lives were brutally taken) far outweighed the kicks in the behind from frustrated constables that would be the most painful reward of the Aldermaston marcher. Yet even in the less dangerous activities of collecting money or promoting discussion the apathy was apparent. Those who cared enough to act were treated with casual disdain by the majority. They were "do-gooders". For the rest, life held other attractions.

We flew into Kentucky after Thanksgiving. The local debates coach quickly revealed himself as a God-is-White-and-Goldwater-is-his-prophet apostle. A Westerner by birth (he came from Iowa) he was a Southerner in belief. We had discovered that by and large debates coaches were on the far left of the liberal wing; and our incautiously angled questions about the colour issue provoked a burst of rightish invective. "Yes, our college was integrated about eight years ago. But that doesn't mean much. You won't find white students going to dances with Negroes or anything; and there's not much inter-racial social life of any kind here. All the Civil Rights legislation in the world won't change the way people think. The compulsion only makes it worse—too many people talk about it all. They're the ones who are making a problem." The star of the basket ball team that night was a Negro. "Colour doesn't mean much in sport when your side's winning," said the boy in the next seat, expressing our own unspoken thoughts.

America is very Mississippi conscious; and Mississippi is very self-conscious. "This'll be the day of your tour that the folks back home will ask you most about;" they said it many times, and they were right. We passed above the southern landscape, a flat terrain, sparsely wooded, with sandy roads, and turbid sinuous yellowing rivers, and made a wind-buffeted landing at Columbus Airport. The conversation quickly turned to the racial question. Jonathan said that last night he'd been involved in a pantie raid. "Well, we can't promise you a race riot, I'm afraid," came the reply. The speech professor, Mr Dudley, was a true progressive, and eager to tell us all we wished to know. From his point of view as a teacher the gut of the problem was that the Negro's was a "starved culture". Inside the houses there were no pictures, books or records. A vicious circle was produced. The Negro was condemned as too backward to be worth equal consideration. But it was because he was denied equal consideration that he was so backward. One of the debaters, a young Goldwaterite, said he wasn't against integration in principle "but not for our children".

We drove around the small southern town of Starksville (pop. 12,000). The passage of the Civil Rights Bill had not erased the visible traces of segregation in hotels and garages, and the professor told us, where the notices "Whites Only" had gone, their spirit was enforced by the local police. Any white who stayed in a Negro hotel was liable to be arrested for trying to provoke a breach of the peace. In education there had been as yet no effort to mix the two races; there was a Negro high school at one end of the town, a white one at the other. Again no one had attempted to assert their rights under the protection of the

136

new bill; nor, thought the professor, would they for quite
a while. To arrive at the Negro ghetto one had to turn off
the high road on to gravel pathways. The dwelling places
were lifted straight from any film set of Caldwell land. They
were wooden shacks, patched with posters for the most part.
Dogs and chickens ran loose in the streets. The children
playing in the dust looked at us curiously for the moment
and then turned away. No one seemed to own a car around
there. Next to this area we saw new apartment blocks for
Negroes, provided on a means test basis by the Federal
Government—a bridgehead in the war on depression. But
even the churches are segregated. "I believe it's the same
God," said the professor wryly. There is much still that
could but won't go with the wind.

We returned to our rooms faced with a problem. Before
we had come to America, we had decided that we could not
speak at a segregated university. But our researches into
the status of Mississippi State University had been faulty.
Technically it was not segregated. Indeed had it been, this
would have been in violation of the law. But the admissions
system demanded that any prospective student be sponsored by five alumni of the university. Given the regional
intake this was just another way of saying "No Negroes".
None had tried, still less succeeded, to break down the
barriers. It was the technique of the fraternities, applied on
a wider scale. So what to do? To pull out now would be
gratuitously insulting. It was we who had made the mistake
after all in coming there. To speak, silent on the crucial
issue, would be false to ourselves and to those who sent us.
We compromised with a statement. The speech professor,
whom we phoned, approved our plan as he understood our
dilemma. Any help to the liberal cause was welcome. We

must confess that it was with a certain nervousness that we sat down to supper at the fraternity house. Michael's neighbour turned to him and said, "Well, and what do you think of us racially prejudiced old Southerners?" The charm of the Southern accent is bewitching, and the effect of the generous hospitality (not for nothing do Americans apply the epithet "Southern" to hospitality as readily as we apply the word "Gallic" to charm) muted any desire to argue. We talked in vague and general terms. One boy made an interesting statement to the effect that it was surprising how even in the South the news of Kennedy's assassination had been received with dismay—a reversal of the usual comment. At coffee before the debate Michael spoke to another debate coach and his wife, who had moved down South from Illinois. He talked of the difficulties and challenges of being a liberal on the faculty. In his classes the sons of rich planters provided a core of old style racists against whom he would argue constantly. But the atmosphere was always one of tension. Because of his beard he was apparently constantly suspected of being a Civil Rights worker (the indices of disreputability are clearly the same on both sides of the Atlantic), and once, when on holiday in Louisiana, he had been trailed by a police car for a hundred miles.

The debate that night before a packed hall of two hundred or so people was on the United Nations topic. Jonathan, who spoke first, rose and said:

"First of all, on behalf of Michael Beloff and myself, I'd like to say how glad we are to be debating here at Mississippi State and to thank you very much for your kind hospitality and welcome.

"Before I debate this resolution, there is one thing that I

feel must be said and I say it on behalf of both of us from Oxford.

"Michael and I come to you tonight as representatives of Oxford University and of the Oxford Union Society. The Oxford Union has, on many occasions, passed resolutions condemning racial discrimination in any form, and both of us have wholeheartedly supported these resolutions. So I'm sure you'll understand that we feel we have a duty and trust to the Oxford Union.

"We have no wish needlessly to involve ourselves in local politics. But since we have found ourselves in what, contrary to all the earlier information we received, is an all white university, we feel that we must make it clear that our visit does not, in any way, express approval of the policies of segregation.

"We owe it to Oxford to make this statement as we owe it to you to proceed with this debate."

Silence from the audience. And then into the old routine —and what in fact turned out to be a remarkably good debate. But the reactions at the reception afterwards were mixed. Most applauded our statements; and even when they disagreed with the sentiments approved our motives in expressing them. Some even thought that it might be of genuine use. Three fifteen-year-old high-school boys shook our hands and tearfully thanked us for "daring to stand up for their cause". But there were many contrary and hostile remarks. One woman suggested that we had meant it all as a joke, "You can't really believe that we're all segregationalists. Still, we'll forgive you this once." Others showed quite clearly why it had not been a joke. One faculty member said that the remarks were "totally unnecessary and uncalled for". Another argued that the University

139

was already totally de-segregated in attitude—whatever that meant. Among the students, attitudes were mixed. One defended "separate development" as the best solution, and spoke bitterly of the FBI as the "Federal Bureau of Integration". One girl was passionately opposed to mixed marriages, having watched mixed dating at Colorado University and found it "disgusting". (We only once met a mixed couple on a campus in the whole tour—a studied contrast to England.) Some were all equivocations and compromises; it wasn't a question of colour, merely of education, intelligence or tradition. Some were frank extremists. "Those boys in Philadelphia (the three murdered Civil Rights workers) got what they deserved." "The man who should get the Nobel Peace prize is Governor Wallace, not Martin Luther King." Argument was difficult when one shared little common ground. Perhaps most surprising of all was the attitude of the College Dean who said that it was kind of us to come at all, feeling as we did. Apparently had we refused to speak altogether no one would have been surprised. Mississippi expected her boycotts.

We left the next morning at dawn. The last word of our charming and hospitable debates partner of the night before was: "There's a lot of ignorant people who come down here to put things right that they don't understand about at all." The local newspaper printed flattering reviews of our speeches, said that we had found the campus architecture among the most remarkable and attractive of any we had seen (as indeed we had) and mentioned nothing of our protest. So much for the value of dissent in a closed society!

That was really the end of our contact with overt racialism in the South. In a bus station in northern Florida we noticed that Whites and Negroes sat at separate ends of the waiting room, and on separate stools at the counter. Old habits die hard. But for Jonathan there came a far more revealing insight into the Southern mentality. As he was escorting some young blonde back to the campus he found his flow of sweet nothings interrupted by an anxious "My God, we're in coloured town, let's run". When he asked why, she said that any American white boy finding himself in coloured town (this was in Gainesville) would run away. Apparently there had been no actual incidents of interracial clashes. There was simply this persistent feeling that there was something alien and dangerous about the Negro area of the town. Jonathan, with English sang-froid and an unfitness engendered by years of good living, preferred to walk, and survived to tell the tale, farcical if it weren't a little frightening.

In Hampton, Virginia, we debated at an all Negro university. We arrived late at the airport on a clear sunlit day, and were met by two Negro students, a boy and a girl, who drove us along the shore past the bathing huts and sailing boats that coloured the sky towards the campus. Our conversation was casual, ordinary. We felt, perhaps as always, that we should be asking grandiloquent questions about the human conditions or their views on the future, but we felt, perhaps as always, that it was not for us to take such initiatives.

At the campus we were treated no differently from anywhere else. There was no particular urge to impress us with "Negro achievements". And indeed the campus itself was not distinct in style from any other campus except that all the faces were black. Clearly it was bounti-

141

fully endowed from private sources. There was no sense in which it could be urged that in this case segregation had meant inferiority.

We debated on the United Nations. Jonathan's partner was a graduate student from Sierra Leone, Michael's an American Negro from Tennessee, who had been born in but "escaped" from Mississippi. The debate was a peculiarly limp one. The issue itself aroused little feeling among the audience; and on that evening it was doubtful that the debaters did much to create any. But question time was altogether a different matter. No longer did the future of the Beatles or the National Health Service hold sway.

"What do the Oxford team think of the situation in South Africa?"

"What are the British going to do about Southern Rhodesia?"

"How did you make out in Mississippi?"

"What do the people in England think about the race issue in America?"

It was in many ways a pity that we had to adjourn to see the play!

And so we crossed back over the Mason Dixon line and headed up North for the last stage of our tour. Looking back with a sense of perspective we find it difficult to say anything by way of conclusion. We had, after all, kept to the highways of American society. Education is supposed to erode prejudice. Redneck reaction should be the prerogative of the ignorant and the untaught. Our experience, where it hadn't been visual, had been at second hand. And yet it had made this bitter and lasting impression. We shall best remember one thing. The bulk of the tour took place in the wake of the British elections, and time after time Americans would ask us about the result at Smethwick.

"Could you tell us about the English race problem?"

"How do you intend to cope with integration in your cities?"

There was a wish to expose a confession that we shared this problem, to saddle us with our portion of the guilt. At the start we were apt to apologise a little; to say that there would be many red faces among British Liberals today of those who had been too quick to condemn the Americans across the Atlantic. But gradually it became clear that comparisons were not odious, just meaningless. The scale of the question was different. In England at the Establishment level there was no debate; all shared a more or less liberal attitude. In America the division in society was reflected in the debate at its summit. And at the end this was the point we used again and again. But till the end there was an uneasy feeling that maybe this was not our argument.

In New York two days before we left Michael took a taxi from Forty-Second street. The driver was wearing a kind of helmet. "Why?" Michael asked. "In case some fool asks me to drive into the nigger district."

9

Home Straight

By THE beginning of December we had reached the southern tip of Florida and started heading homewards up the East Coast.

Florida itself provided us with some interesting experiences. At Florida State University we were debating on the same night as a fundamentalist preacher, Carl McIntyre. Students had to choose between a comic sermon on the evils of admitting Red China to the United Nations, or the equally comic attraction of the well-known Oxford socialite (*sic*) Michael Beloff, on "Why America Needs a Welfare State". It was not surprising that both functions were poorly attended.

We flew on to St Petersburg. Oscar Wilde once said, "When good Americans die they go to Paris." St Petersburg has supplanted Paris. It is the city of old people and undertakers. Walking along the beaches less than ten per cent of the promenaders we saw were under the age of seventy-five, and of those ten per cent half were fat and prosperous morticians who had retired in their early thirties on their profits.

We were the guests of Florida Presbyterian College, a university founded less than five years ago through the

144

munificence of Southern Presbyterian churches and local donors. In fact, it was a university with financial problems, since many Southern Presbyterian churches had withdrawn their support after the college had been integrated. Also, the college could not possibly afford to offend the local donors in matters of policy, and as a result no left wing speakers were allowed on to the campus.

This college had been founded, so the President of the University told us, "To promote purposeful Christianity. We want to wake up students' minds to asking and answering profound questions about Christianity." We discovered that all members of the faculty are extremely enthusiastic about this "purposeful Christianity" business. Indeed, during a two-hour dinner with some of the professors we discussed no other subject except Christianity. Alas, this celestial enthusiasm is not shared by the students, who despite having to go through a compulsory freshman course on Western civilisation (which is supposed to inject purposeful Christianity into everyone's mind), are no more and no less enthusiastic about being Christians than students in any other university.

The only external symptom of all this emphasis on religion was the existence of a student organisation known as the Honour Court. The Honour Court was originally set up by the high-minded faculty in the belief that students who committed a sin would be so keen to repent that they would come publicly to weekly sessions of the Honour Court, declare their transgressions and receive forgiveness. In practice, however, the Honour Court, to start with, never had anything to do because no students apparently seemed anxious publicly to receive forgiveness for the sins that everyone knew were going on. But after a few words

145

by the zealous President, this reluctance for personal repentance was replaced by an enthusiasm for getting repentance out of someone else. A corps of public-spirited students was established who felt honour bound to report the crimes committed by other students. Once a few people had been reported by *their* enemies, they were quick to retaliate by reporting crimes committed by their enemies. By the time we arrived the guards were so busy guarding themselves that there was a secret police atmosphere all over the campus. The experience of Florida Presbyterian College bodes ill for those who wish at Oxford to replace the Proctors by a Student Council as the source of discipline and authority.

We advanced northwards to the University of Florida at Gainesville. Here we were met by two seventeen-year-olds who explained that they were to debate against us although in fact, they had never actually debated in their lives before. When asked why they had been selected for the evening's debate they explained that all the regular debaters had been banned from taking any part in campus activities owing to the fact that they had indulged in "red eye".

This completely mystified us and we decided all the debate team must have been in a punch-up, getting an unpleasant battering to their faces which was one degree worse than black eye. However, subsequent investigation proved that "red eye" was, in fact, the habit of revealing your unclothed posterior to ladies in the street, a Southern version of "mooning" though done in anger rather than sport. The debates team, annoyed by the decision in a tournament of a neighbouring university's female debates coach, had perpetrated "red eye" in her direction after the

146

tournament and this had been punished by exclusion from the Oxford debate.

After leaving Florida, where we had bathed in warm December seas, played touch football on gleaming sands, and dawdled among the palms, we headed up to North Carolina and the incipient rigours of winter. Duke and Wake Forest, which we visited, are colleges founded through the munificence of local cigarette millionaires, who established these centres of learning in much the same spirit as the mediaeval barons founded monasteries—to expiate their sins in this world and lay up credit for the next. The students, while addicted to macabre jokes about the source of their good fortune, smoked neither more nor less than their average compatriots.

Our final port of call before New York was Philadelphia, the city where all American troubles started. With dutiful smiles we did the required tour of Independence Hall and adjacent buildings. Jonathan distinguished himself on this occasion by remarking that he had always thought that Liberty Belle was George Washington's mistress. As we discovered, the spirit of freedom that characterises the history of the city is not extinguished. There are still today, as there have always been, Philadelphians watchful for the subversive influence of foreign ideas and it was here that we at last had an opportunity to visit a headquarters of the John Birch Society. It was located in an establishment called "The American Freedom Bookstall". This was one of the comic highspots of our tour. When one got inside the bookstall it turned out to be a shoe shop with a few books on shelves where there were no shoes. The proprietor of both enterprises was a wizened little cobbler who looked as though he might have escaped from a nearby lunatic asylum. He was bald, except for one luxuriant wisp of sand-coloured hair which sprouted from the middle of his head and was strewn all over the rest of his head in thin wisps. He had a wild, hunted look in his eyes which was given added effect by the way he was hammering away at his last with the demonaic energy of one who stamps out Communism for a hobby. At the same time, he was muttering weird right wing slogans sotto voce.

Jonathan edged up to the only other individual in the shop and asked him what was really good among the pamphlets.

"Everything is great in this shop," he beamed. "What are you particularly interested in?"

"Propaganda techniques," came the ambiguous reply.

"Say, you're from England, aren't you, that's great. Say, Harry, here's a guy who will spread the truth in England for us."

Jonathan solemnly shook hands with the cobbler who spread a wealth of Birchite pamphlets before him. One of them claimed that Britain was eighty per cent Communist controlled. We politely suggested that the figures might be a little inaccurate, since Communism had at the most a one per cent following in England.

"Not at all," said the cobbler, his voice rising. "Look at that new government of yours."

"But they're Socialists, not Communists."

"Socialists are Communists," quoth the cobbler, thumping his last. "Who are you, anyway?"

Michael, who is a real live Socialist, feared he might be lynched if he revealed his true identity and melted away behind a pile of old shoes.

Jim Galeese, our host, spoke up, "Mr Aitken's a real English Conservative."

The cobbler had heard of this subversive cell. "All English Conservatives support the Welfare State, don't they?"

"Broadly speaking, yes."

"Then they're Communists too."

To fill in our knowledge of who was and who wasn't a Communist we then played a quiz game to distinguish the cops from the robbers.

Harold Wilson and Hubert Humphrey were predictably Communists of the worst type. Hard on their heels came General Eisenhower. The late President Kennedy and Sir Alec Douglas-Home had dangerous Communist sympathies. Who then were the non-Communists?

Richard Nixon was a real good guy. Senator Barry Goldwater was a knight in shining armour. Alongside them were General Franco and Dr Salazar of Portugal. Spain, Portugal and Switzerland were, in fact, the only countries in the world which seemed to have less than fifty per cent Communists. Britain seventy per cent. Canada and the United States both had between seventy-five and eighty-five per cent Communists.

The political discussion seemed to be getting nowhere, so we asked some questions about the movement.

"How large was it?"

"Our membership is secret, but it's growing all the time and is now very big and very powerful."

"How is it financed?"

"By contributions from members."

"What do you have to do to join?"

"That's a secret until you really want to join, but you

149

have to swear allegiance to the flag, to preserving the true Constitution."

Finally, we tried to acquire some literature. On being given several pamphlets we started to walk out of the shop, thinking that these were free handouts. Not so. "That'll be $1.85." This seemed an exorbitant price for such a load of rubbish so we asked if we could be given some of them free.

"Certainly not," cried the cobbler, his voice rising with passion and indignation. "Don't you realise that that's the sort of thing we are fighting against? The Welfare State and its giving of something for nothing!"

We bought two pamphlets for 25 cents and walked out, glad to find freedom outside the bookstall.

In the evening the British Consul in Philadelphia entertained us to dinner. It was the first time we had been in the social company of a compatriot for three months, and the sardonic wit of our urbane proconsular host and some of his guests made us reflect on the big difference between British and American conversation.

American conversation is rather like a cricket match in that one man goes in to bat, scores all the runs he can and then makes way for someone else to do the same. Thus at American dinner tables monologue follows monologue, and although the listeners occasionally try to bowl a googly in the shape of a tricky question or sharp contradiction, a skilful monologuist can hold his own against all comers, and only when he has exhausted his vocal chords will he declare his innings closed. He is then followed by someone else whose intention is clearly to outdo the previous speaker in eloquence, erudition, volume and length of monologue. The hostess acts as umpire, giving a speaker "out" when he is no longer holding the company's interest, and arranging whose turn it is to monologue next. The guests who are not trying to catch the speaker out and so get their chance to talk, merely throw in words of encouragement such as "Gee, that's fascinating" or "How marvellous" and are the equivalent of MCC members in the pavilion at Lords who applaud fine strokes with a "Jolly well played, sir!"

British conversation resembles much more closely the game of tennis. Dinner party talk often begins with a fast service in the shape of a provocative question. If the object of the questioning is worth his invitation he slams back a fast return. The conversation is then taken up by all the guests, and if the guests are on form there will be good brisk contributions from everyone, with quick repartee the essence of the chatter.

These differences in national conversational habits were displayed to the full at the British Consul's dinner party. For example, at one moment in the evening the director of a local Federal Agency held forth at length on the subject of how his agency would have altered its entire policy if Goldwater had won the election. Finally declaring his innings closed, the director settled into his chair for the next monologue, asking the British Consul: "Did your Government issue you with any instructions to be carried out if Goldwater won?"

"Instructions for evacuation do you mean?" replied Her Majesty's Consul, as his English guests dissolved in laughter.

On the whole we did not suffer unduly from the normal tedium of American conversation, simply because we were usually the guests of honour at meals, and could

151

break up potential long-distance talkers by asking frequent questions. Indeed, by forcing Americans to play British conversational tennis, even if with their own cricket bats, we managed to acquire a lot of information in a short time and to make our social discussions live up to Oscar Wilde's dictum that "conversation should touch on everything and concentrate on nothing".

However, there were all too many occasions where, due to the presence of two or three loquacious professors, we were forced to endure American conversation in the classic form described earlier. Cricket has been defined as "a game created to give an impression of the concept of eternity" and the same is, alas, painfully true of American conversation.

And so on to New York for our two final engagements. The first was with the English Speaking Union where we discussed the momentous resolution "Frailty Thy Name is Woman" before an audience composed largely of English expatriates. Oratorically speaking the White Cliffs of Dover were in sight. Our jokes were greeted neither with frenzied hysteria nor with incomprehending silence. Our opponents were an engineer and an advertising agent, both of whom had emigrated from Britain twenty years ago. Their jokes were of the same vintage. As we munched tea cakes and scones with the good ladies of the English Speaking Union after the debate we might have been speakers at a WI meeting with the strains of "Jerusalem" fading in our ears, being entertained and thanked for a little talk which was so very, very English.

However, nostalgia was soon dispelled by our final engagement which could hardly have been more American. We were to debate at the United States Merchant Marine

Academy, King's Point, New York. As a harbinger of this function we were sent a sinister piece of paper headed "Regimental Memorandum". This was apparently written in code, since apart from our names and a few other phrases vaguely recognisable as the English language this memorandum consisted entirely of extraordinary figures, initials and symbols. For example, under a paragraph headed "Schedule" there was the cryptic sentence: 2010—4th CL Sections muster march Bowd Aud. Report ROOW. LCDR. VJ. Lugowski USMSOIC.

When we finally cracked the cipher and, with the help of the chauffeur who drove us to King's Point, de-coded the message, it transpired that we were to attend a Christmas Dinner before the debate, and a musical interlude during it.

The Dinner was a gargantuan twelve-course repast, containing items such as "One Whole Premium Turkey per Cadet table, Home Style with Country dressing"; "Candied Yams" and "Old Fashioned Pumpkin Pie".

To judge by their appetites on this occasion the young Merchant Mariners had never had a square meal in their lives, for conversation was actively discouraged in order that full attention could be given to beating one's neighbour in the race for second helpings.

After everyone had gorged themselves to the full and the mainbrace had been spliced in apple cider, a reverent silence was accorded to the Admiral of the Merchant Marine Academy who read out his Christmas message to the assembled company. Entitled "A Star to Steer By", the message contained the interesting theological innovation that the Star in the East was spotted by the Israelite Navy long before the Shepherds and the Wise Men saw it.

Why nobody had ever related this interesting historical fact before did not concern the cadets who all nodded their heads appreciatively at the Admiral's revelation.

After the gastronomic festivities finally came to an end, amidst much stamping of feet and saluting, the thousand-odd cadets mustered and marched to the Bowditch Auditorium. We solemnly marched with them and, thanks to the apple cider, we found it comparatively easy to roll with a true nautical gait. However, our expertise in merchant marine matters was soon exposed when, after arriving on the platform, we were told by the officer in charge "Take the port table, Oxford". Landlubbers to the core, we of course went to the wrong side, Jonathan doing his best to cover up by saying "Sorry, I only saw water in the decanter on the other table".

For the second time in the evening the Admiral delivered a speech, this time about the traditions of the Merchant Navy and the history of Oxford University, subjects on which he was respectively vaguely eloquent, and eloquently vague. His remarks were followed by a brisk orgy of bell ringing which we took to mean "seconds out of the ring" but which in fact only signified that the time was "six bells" (nine o'clock).

We were next treated to a musical display by the Academy's brass band, who performed hornpipes and sea shanties, followed by a rather ironic version of "Rule Britannia". Then finally the debate got under way. For the forty-sixth and last time we ran through the routine of old jokes and old arguments, enlivened only by a Whitehall farce scene when the chairman announced, "I now call on Cadet Roloff to speak". Michael, whose ears by this time were tuned for even the most bizarre mispronunciation of

154

his name, assumed that he had been awarded a naval title for the evening, and so sprang to his feet and marched head high to the rostrum. The genuine Cadet Roloff did the same, with the result that both Beloff and Roloff collided simultaneously with the podium, like two *Titanics* hitting an iceberg.

A few minutes later we were listening to the last Vote of Thanks, and munching our last sausage roll at our last post-debate reception. Then we were free men. In three months we had come to like America and the Americans enormously, despite our immense amusement at their national absurdities. But it was equally true that the visit had bred in us a deeper respect for the standards and values of the country to which we were returning.

10

Not So Much an Education,
More a Way of Life

MICHAEL AMBLED across the sunlit slope of the campus at Bates College, Maine, and into the Senior Faculty Room. All along the tour Americans had expressed themselves anxious that we should share the pleasures of the classroom, and Michael, smitten by the blonde charms of his girl guide, had unanimously decided to offer himself up as a guinea pig. "Let's see if we've got anything to fit you," she said, as if she were offering him a choice of sports jackets rather than of classes to attend. "There's Latin, English literature—I don't suppose you want to be bothered with that. . . . You might try Professor M. though. He's just started on the Philosophy of History course."

"Glad to have you with us, Mike," said the Professor. All the teachers seemed to be Professor. Merit, not title, differentiates them in the eyes of their students. The class took some time to assemble, streaming in from all sides of the campus in their tee shirts and jeans, pony tails and crew cuts, acknowledging the presence of their teacher with an easy "Hiya Frank". We all sat round somewhat rickety tables. "Well, Dave," said the Professor, "I guess we'd better hear that paper of yours on 'Truth and Fact in

156

History'." There was a lot of coy chatter from Dave as if he had been asked to play a minuet at a Victorian Christmas party, and throughout his hurried reading he interspersed mock modest comments like "Gee, this ain't much good". Another student, Sam, was appointed inquisitor-in-chief and would break in with frequent contradiction. After twenty minutes of what at times developed into a Crosby–Hope routine rather than a Socratic dialogue the question was thrown open to the floor. There was a lot of joshing and joke-making. Most of the class, about twenty in all, were smoking. One girl knitted, her furrowed concentration ambiguously directed throughout. After a while Professor M. in his capacity as referee called "Break", and for the remaining few minutes read to us from various contemporary accounts of the Louisiana purchase to show how each participant had his own version of what had happened. Then after a short speech in summation he dispersed the class.

We cannot claim that this cosy experience is really typical for, in general, Americans carry to education the passion for size that distinguishes so much of what they do. The first thing we noticed about American education was that there was a lot of it. Boston is reputed to have as many colleges as Paris has brothels. There is, of course, great variety among the institutions. One typical establishment of higher education is the Liberal Arts College, such as Bates in Maine, or Hiram, Wooster, and Denison in Ohio. As far as we could judge the connection with either liberalism or artiness was small, but an atmosphere of scholarship was more easily created on these small self-contained campuses which often housed as few as eight hundred students. Akin to these in size were the sectarian schools:

Catholic colleges like La Salle or St Josephs in Philadelphia, presided over by quick talking Jesuits with a good line in Irish ancestry and American jokes; or Protestant institutions like Eastern Nazarene, Boston, and Florida Presbyterian, with their somewhat tight-lipped approach to debates and life alike. At the other end of the scale were the huge State universities, like Ohio State, towns of some thirty thousand students, anonymous, sprawling, diverse. In between in size ranked the aristocratic colleges of the Ivy League, the rich uncles, and the Teachers' Training Colleges, the poor cousins, of the system.

What all these institutions shared, and where they differed from at least the older English universities, was the concept of the Campus. Whether it was the red stone and white bricked buildings of the Liberal Arts Colleges or the bulky grey concrete edifices of the State universities their architecture was concentrated in one area. Sometimes, too, as in the Liberal Arts Colleges that we visited in Ohio, there would be nothing but scattered hamlets in the vicinity, and the nearest big town would be many miles away. In this they differ from almost every English university. Universities in America are self-contained, even self-centred. This naturally affects the attitudes of the students and often divorces them from life outside the campus. It may be a contributory factor to the general lack of political and social commitment which is discussed in the next chapter. On the other hand, especially in the smaller universities, it certainly creates a sense of community and should, in theory at any rate, promote undistracted intellectual achievement.

The second factor that these colleges share, and that ours lack, is wealth. The libraries, always the centre-piece

158

of any aspirant institution of learning, overwhelmed us everywhere with their munificence. The smallest Liberal Arts colleges would have libraries containing not only many thousands of books, but periodicals, magazines and newspapers from all over the world. And some of the libraries, like the Rare Books Library at Yale, or the Law Library at Harvard (which has, for example, a whole section devoted to the Law of Mediaeval Bulgaria) are among the greatest libraries of the world. At the other end of the spectrum of university activity we found much to admire in the way of sports facilities: the football stadia of the Midwestern State universities that would dwarf Highbury or White Hart Lane; indoor gymnasia for the basketball team; rows of tennis courts for all weathers; rooms for massage and heat treatment. To give but one example: at Denison, Ohio, a college of less than fifteen hundred students, we found not only an athletics outdoor track, set deep in a small valley so that the hills around acted as natural windbreaks, but also an indoor track (how many are there in all Britain?), and an Olympic sized swimming pool (again, how many has Britain got?). No one could really believe us when we explained that Oxford University had neither a swimming pool nor gymnasium to call its own. "But it's the most famous university in the world," they would say. The Midwestern universities are so rich that they even employ teams of research workers to gather material for their debates squad, and computers to analyse the possible courses of argument. Individual tape recorders for language students, closed circuit television for the larger classes, soundproof rooms for the experiments in the Speech Departments, model theatres for the drama students, printing presses

159

for the embryo journalists, these are commonplace. At Purdue, Indiana, is the largest theatre in the world with an auditorium that can seat six thousand. Ohio State university has not only its own television service, but also its own airport. For apart from State and federal subsidies and the accumulation of fees, the legacies and endowments given by alumni to their old colleges are often huge. The American cherishes the memory of his college days with the affection that in England is bestowed more frequently on the school. "I'm a Ball State Teachers' Training College man," one would hear someone say with pride, much as he might say in England, "I'm an Old Rugbeian".

The average American student thus lives in a seclusion that is often aesthetic; sleeps in dormitories with individual rooms, which will certainly have central heating and electric razor points, and in the more modern ones like those at Murray State, Kentucky, will run to showers and lavatories; eats in large cafeterias where the food, if not suited to the gourmet, at least satisfies the gourmand; has snack bars and soda fountains to satiate his extra-curricular appetites, and usually possesses every facility for study, sport and hobby that could be desired. (The one caveat might be about the degree of privacy obtainable.) Yet in the university land of milk and honey, the milk is turning sour and the honey is losing its sweetness.

It is clear that American education is undergoing a crisis similar in intensity, if different in kind, to that experienced in our own country. And yet the American university system possesses most of the features that appear to the radical educationalist in England most desirable: comprehensive schools; widespread rather than élite education beyond them; the equality of status of colleges of tech-

160

nology in the title of the degrees that they confer with the older established universities; syllabuses that break down the barriers between the two cultures; and syllabuses of a practical slant that draw on materials which in England would not be considered ripe for academic study at all. It was somewhat startling to discover that what we might have considered Utopia was considered by so many Americans to be Purgatory.

The root of the trouble is that it has proved impossible to maintain élite standards of education for a mass student population. The greatest difference that our conversations unearthed between the methods of teaching on either side of the Atlantic.was the degree of professorial control over the studies of his pupils. During one week in our tour in early November our audiences suddenly fell off drastically as on campus after campus we hit the doldrums of the half-term exam days. One afternoon at Bates we were deserted by all our hosts as it was a "No Cut Class" day. The question that was most frequently posed to Michael, who had missed a term at Oxford to come on the tour, was not "How are you going to find time to make up the work?" but "How are you going to find time to make up your grades?" One's progress is apparently gauged by the number of classes one attends, not by the amount of knowledge that one imbibes. The concurrent passion for classification by examiners is of course anathema to anyone who believes that education is more than a matter of marks scored. In England we try to avoid this at the university level until the final degree. But in America, the teachers confessed, the large bulk of their classes have not the intellectual maturity or personal responsibility to be allowed to pursue their own course of studies with the

161

same freedom that is enjoyed by their English counterparts. Examinations are used as much to weed out the weaker students as to evaluate the standards of the better ones. "The dormitories are absolutely crammed here at the moment," said the speech professor at Ball State Teachers' Training College, "but come the summer semester maybe as many as fifty per cent will have dropped out. The wastage is enormous."

Another result of the invasion of the universities by swarms of semi-educated American boys and girls is the dilution of the syllabuses. This has two aspects. One is the introduction of courses, whose stimulus to mental activity is less than exiguous. The Schools of Journalism, of Business, of Speech, these are all admirable institutions in which America has pioneered an impressive route. But at a lower level a high sounding glossary conceals a multitude of idiocies. Domestic Economics (egg boiling *et al.*); Industrial Arts (carpentry); Driver Education (the syllabus of a British school of motoring). At one college in Florida we saw young gymnasts hurling themselves around on trapezes and trampolines and were told that they were graduates of the school of Circusology, presumably doing their homework. At Michigan State in the Kellog Centre, where we stayed, the waiters and room service stewards were all students engaged in becoming hoteliers. No one would dispute the value of training in all these matters; but whether a degree in them can be considered equal to a degree in some of the more established subjects is questionable. The fact is, though, that the Americans take these outward marks so seriously that in some places one cannot merely graduate, but even take a doctorate in these courses. More means not just worse, but positively awful.

162

The second aspect is the shunning of specialisation. Undergraduate courses in American universities are broadly based. Now if the purpose of this was to produce a race of Renaissance men, versed in all manner of subjects and cultures, it would be a worthy ideal. (It is easy to poke fun at some of the blinkered and ageing syllabuses that are taught in *our* older universities.) But that is not the purpose. These courses are not meant to accommodate the capable and the intelligent, but the backward and unintellectual. A little learning is a dangerous thing, and the average American student has a lot of little learning. There is moreover often no attempt to encourage a careful choice. A rapid course in World Culture will be followed by two years spent in the study of, say, Trigonometry, Moral Philosophy, and French Literature. Indeed, the American college student is more often than not pursuing in his undergraduate days a course of study that is no more advanced or demanding than that followed by the English schoolboy preparing for the Advanced Certificate of Education.

Another result of the massive university expansion is the growth of the Factories of Learning. These are predominantly a West Coast phenomenon, but as, for example, we found at Ohio State not exclusively so. The sense of anonymity that this produced among the students was apparent. There are, it must be remembered, no colleges of the Oxford–Cambridge type to give the students a greater opportunity for contact with their professors or a greater chance to live a truly communal life. "There are three great examples of mass production in the USA today," said one student to Michael. "At the stockyards in Chicago you can put in a pig at one end of a machine

163

and get a sausage at the other. In the Ford works at Detroit you can put in a piece of metal ore at one end and get an auto at the other. And at a big State university you can put in an ignorant college kid at one end and get an ignorant graduate at the other." These students are often selected by computer, taught by disembodied figures from television screens, working with books which have been systematically filleted for examination purposes ("You could have a shorter *Othello* at one of these places that would cut out Iago," said a boy at Madison, Wisconsin) and lecture notes from lectures that they never went to but whose gist has been processed and sold in the college shops. This is a not very brave new world run riot.

A problem common to all spheres of higher education (though less prevalent in rich private institutions) is a shortage of teachers. "There's a kind of Gresham's law at work; bad teachers driving out good," said the speech professor at Edinboro' State Teacher's Training College, Erie, Penn. "And you get worse and worse people coming into teaching nowadays. They'd rather take any course than this." But of course the need must be supplied however poorly. "You can see the future," said one professor to Jonathan, "Half the population will end up teaching the other half."

The source of all the evil is the prevalent myth that every child born in the USA should have a college education, if it is possible. Constituents believe it, so the State legislators must. Employers believe it, so therefore must potential employees. A college degree is no longer an added qualification for a profession: it is an indispensable one. But of course not everyone is taken in by the mere production of a BA. Those people who in England inveigh against the "inferior status" of Colleges of Advanced Technology and Redbricks could do well to look at the American experience. The fact of conferring the title of university deceives no one. Until the value of the degree given by the new foundation can fairly be equated with that given by older ones, nothing has been achieved. The question now asked in America is not "Have you got a degree?" but "Where did you get your degree from?" or "What sort of a degree have you got?" Everyone knows that a BA in sharkfishing from the University of Miama is worth less than a BA in Liberal Arts from the University of Chicago and certainly less than the Harvard LLB.

The end product of all this is that well-known New World personality, the perpetual student. It is after all the most talented student who suffers the most from a system that panders to the least gifted. He is hampered in his academic enthusiasms by amorphous courses that he cannot bite on, by perpetual examinations that are only a source of irritation, by the company of colleagues who if literate are often barely so. ("I can't even get my kids to spell straight," said one disheartened faculty man at Kent State. "And I'm meant to be teaching them ethics.") At La Salle, Philadelphia, one of the debaters was on the Dean's list, which gave him the rare privilege of exemption from certain exams and permission to work more on his own. This kind of privilege would have been welcomed by many of the students whom we met, but the concept of differentiation is one that is born hard in the American mind. Thus, fettered by a system that has held him back since his school days (it was again alarming to hear teacher after teacher blame the comprehensive idea for the low standards of college freshmen), the gifted student is forced

165

to take more and more higher degrees not only for the purposes of obtaining the first worthwhile and challenging course of education that he has ever received, but also to satisfy the demands of talent-scout employers. An English student who takes an advanced degree is usually training himself for an academic career; no such conclusion could be drawn in the case of his transatlantic counterpart. Five, seven, nine year college students—these were everywhere. But it is by no means certain that every country could afford either to educate or to dispense with the abilities of their best brains for so long.

Fortunately, most American graduate courses bear as little relation to undergraduate ones as a butterfly bears to a caterpillar. At this level at last the benefits of equipment and libraries, of imaginative breakthroughs into new fields of study, bear fruit. The testimony of Americans was less revealing than that of the numerous foreigners whom we met—in both East and Midwest—from India, Germany, Nigeria, England, who claimed that the facilities and the teaching were superb and unrivalled. The experiences of those in the big law schools, Yale, Chicago, Columbia, were especially interesting to us as would-be lawyers. Not for them the esoteric ventures into obscure points of jurisprudence or the glossing of fragments of the Justinianic code. Theirs was a diet that was fed by practical study of tax statutes, company and union law. They would be more likely to be attending seminars on the problems raised in International Law by the invention of the Atom Bomb in the twentieth century than those raised by economic blockades in the nineteenth. There was much more mooting, far fewer lectures. This seemed to us to be relevant adaptation of study to contemporary needs.

166

But the glistening snow at the top of the mountain of education should not blind us to the moss-encrusted rock at the bottom. For while society demands that a teenager should be a college boy or girl, while it supplies him or her directly or indirectly with abundant facilities, it will not subsidise his education to the full. This aspect of the American belief in individual initiative is, alas, harmful to the smooth working of their university system. Of all the colleges that we visited, only at Queens in New York was the education wholly free; indeed the public universities of New York are unique in this respect. The result is that the less affluent students are forced to pay their own way through school. In Welfare State Britain no able student needs to work to earn his fees for tuition. Those who do take vacation employment do so to get "pocket-money". But in America many students are holding down jobs at the same time as they are working for their degrees. We found many examples of this. In Bates our rooms were swept out and cleaned by a student who said that his daily duties as janitor made him rise at six in the morning. Michael's date worked during the lunch hour as a college secretary. Naturally this puts a strain on these students; but if we queried the wisdom of this wastage of effort that should for the duration of one's college days be uniquely directed to the purpose in hand, we were told that this was "the American way".

It may be the American way, but the Americans might profit from trying some other. For one obvious result of the work-your-way-through-college principle is that American students by and large have none of that time for extra-curricular or vacation reading that forms the basis of the English students' culture. Michael used to wax lyrical on

167

the subject of the ideal Oxford man, conversant with the literature of his own and other countries, fluent in several languages, a lover of music and the fine arts, who would no more have needed a course in "European Civilisation in Four Lessons" than he would a ticket to Mars. Naturally this figment of his imagination bore about as much relation to the real person as did the American student, to whom he was addressing his remarks, to a Red Indian, but the airy persiflage cloaked a valid point. We believe much more in training than in merely filling the mind.

"I'm after grades, not knowledge," said one wordly-wise sophomore at Monmouth, Ohio. "The semi-educated teaching the wholly uneducatable. That's the future," said one world-weary professor at Akron, Ohio. "We aren't pursuing an ideal any more. It's running away with us." The progressive American teacher and student seems to be seeking just the opposite from his English conterpart; more streaming; more rigorous syllabuses; less sacrifice of the talented on the altar of uniform mediocrity. Whether he will succeed is another matter. But if he fails, it will be because of the power of the myth, not the lack of money. "You might as well give them a BA at birth," said our host at Pittsburgh cynically. With respect to its foremost philosopher, it is impossible any longer to remain Dewey-eyed about the state of American education.

Of course, American students, strictly controlled though their course of study may be, do not spend all their time in classroom or library. Indeed, the interest that the campus takes in the sporting activities of the college teams once more evokes the ideology of the English public school.

High among the rituals of American college life is the Big Football Game. In England the Dark Blue/Light Blue

168

clashes on the Thames or at Twickenham evoke for a brief spasm of time the interests of sports enthusiasts and snobs alike. Beyond that the world of university sport is a closed book, except to the expert. But imagine that the football game between Bangor and Aberystwyth were to be written up in the *Spectator*. Imagine that every Saturday afternoon David Coleman's nasal accents reported to the armchair fans not from Wembley, Aintree or Lords, but from Nottingham or Hull or Brighton University. Imagine that at the end of the gentlemanly encounter at Association Football between Oxford and Cambridge, instead of the teams coming off to a few "Jolly good show, Cambridge", or "Harry toughers, Percy old man", in the sight of millions of televiewers the Oxford captain was seen to be given a cheque for twenty thousand pounds and to sign professional forms for Tottenham Hotspur. Imagine all these things, transpose them, and you will see that college football in America is not so much a game, more a mass industry. Radicals may continue to gripe about the Keble man, who reads (if the notion is not self-contradictory) the honours school of rowing. But in America the young illiterati of the university football world can pass from the amateur to the professional pitch without ever going by way of the classroom or the lecture hall.

But imagine further. Imagine that instead of the audience at the Iffley Road on Saturday afternoons being composed of a hard core of Vincents men, and a scarcely less hard periphery of muscular well-thewed girls, the crowd featured not only John Sparrow, Isaiah Berlin and Alan Taylor, but every pink-cheeked, starry-eyed Somerville maiden, who could discuss with animated zeal the respective merits of the inside break and the dummy scissors.

169

Everyone, but everyone, is at the football game on Saturday.

On November 7th we went to the match between Ohio State (currently ranked second team in the nation) and Pennsylvania State. From early morning the campus was thronged with programme sellers and ticket touts. We were privileged to be taken to the President's lunch party, a weekly occasion to which important local dignitaries and visitors are asked, where the meal was served to us by lovely sorority sisters, amateur bunny girls in their chastely green costumes. Favours were pinned to our lapels, and we readily agreed to join in the applause for the local team.

The stadium was colossal. It held eighty-four thousand spectators and was crammed to capacity. The occasion dwarfed in size even an English Cup Tie. Helicopters whirred in the air above, aiding the mile upon mile of saloon cars converging on the ground. On the stone edifices which divided one part of the terrace from another armed policemen stood immobile against the sky. In sport as in politics Americans cannot bear to let the central feature go unadorned. It must always be the cocktail, never the neat drink. So here again with half-an-hour to go two bands marched on to the field. This was none of your Cup Final Community Singing—"Land of Hope and Glory" organised under the auspices of the *Daily Express*. The bands were in competition almost as much as the football teams. They must have numbered nearly eighty pieces each. Elegant in contrasting primary colours, they paraded up and down the field, marching in formation. At half-time carefully prepared patterns were traced by the musicians, as each band adopted a theme for improvisation. Pennsylvania State described a recent visit to New

170

York by playing tunes from the *World of Suzy Wong* and strutting in the shape of a pagoda. Ohio State paid tribute to the fact that it was Dad's Day by playing what was meant to be fatherly music and making patriarchal shapes. Central to these performances were the drum majors, prancing figures, dressed like hussars without their horses, high stepping it in front and twirling their silver batons like trained jugglers.

Then came the cheer leaders. Evidently we could not be trusted to offer our support unaided. A sextet of handsome gymnasts, three girls, three boys, in the red and white colours of the home team, emerged from the tunnel with a trampoline and started to perform prodigies of leap and somersault. In between the callisthenics they exhorted us with well-trained voices to join in the choruses. "We want touchdowns." "Hold that Line." "Ra Ta Ta Ohio." Optimistic to the last, they twitched and trembled like fishes out of water, their struggles ever fainter as Ohio's chances vanished with the afternoon sun. Occasionally the bands, who had been penned like cattle behind fences fringing the pitch, would burst out with shrill trumpetings and flutings to spur on the gladiators. As spectators we allowed our duties of encouragement to be performed more or less vicariously.

Finally the players ran out on to the field, about ninety a side, armoured from head to foot, a squadron of Dan Dares. Size is of the essence in the American football player, and their natural physique is exaggerated by the padding and helmets. Quite why this padding is necessary we are unaware. The only apparent danger lies in the tackling, which if anything is less dangerous than the tackling in English rugby football since in the American game

171

everyone is tackled at the earliest possible opportunity after the referee's whistle, regardless of whether he has the ball or not. The person to be tackled is only in any danger because of the metal plated covering of his armadillo aggressor. There is clearly some football cold war in progress. Of course, to the uninitiated spectator the whole affair looks potentially as dangerous as a commando raid in Vietnam.

The second thing that one notices is the amount of time that is spent in talking. We thought that we would have been rather good at American football, although quite useless at the English type, since the transatlantic game clearly gives as much prestige to the conversationalist and orator as it does to the athlete. Before each scrum (and scrums seem to take place at two-minute intervals) both sides huddle into separate conclaves for what looks like a good old gossip. The only game that we can think of where two teams spend an equal amount of time in whispering preparation is charades.

We speculated as to what was the subject matter under discussion at each of these conclaves. Sometimes by the posture, grotesquely swollen buttocks up, visor-protected noses impressed to the ground, it seemed as though the players were studying some interesting form of botanical growth. At others, it appeared from the wild gesticulations and nodding of heads as though a political meeting were in progress.

We were disappointed to be informed that these discussions, in fact, always concerned tactics and signals, but from the length of time each consultation takes we were sure that something much more interesting must really be the subject. During a game lasting three hours only one

172

hour will be spent with the ball actually in play, and two hours will be spent talking about these tactics and signals. It all seemed very long-winded to a student of the fast moving ninety minute games of soccer or rugby in England.

After the confabulations the tortoise groups break up, and the huge Goliaths dance away like little girls who have just heard a secret, clapping their hands in glee, and arranging themselves in the customary "off" position. The magic numbers are shouted, there are frenzied movements, about twenty people crash noisily to the ground; and the whole process starts all over again.

A game of American football gives one a vivid impression of what the first World War must have been like; an endless series of bruising encounters, no quarter given, no territory gained. Only in very brief flashes are the defences split open, and touchdowns scored amid wild and persistent cheering, somersaults and musical interludes.

Although only eleven players from each side appeared upon the field at one time, there was copious use of reserves. These would rush on to the field at frequent intervals to replace any individual on whose brow had broken out the smallest bead of sweat or who was in any other way showing the strain of the game. Our favourite player, onomato-poeically named Chunko, hardly appeared on the field at all, but loomed with eighteen-and-a-half stone menace during the whole afternoon on the sidelines like the ultimate deterrent.

The most diverting episode of the afternoon from our point of view was the half-time interval, when the choice of the Dad of Dad's was announced. At the appearance of this small man in a grey flannel suit, the Ohio apotheosis of paternity, the stadium rocked with applause. For a moment we were transported from the world of the demi-gods to the world of men.

American football has something in it of chess, though with of course live players. The dominant figure is the coach who conducts the whole strategy of the match, keeping in constant telephonic communication with a spy in the sky, high up on the summit of the terrace. The football coach ranks slightly above the College President in the hierarchy of the Midwestern university. Farther east in the urbane Atlantic coastline football is treated with a more mature sense of proportion. The only other football game we saw was between Harvard and Columbia. The stadium contained only about twelve thousand spectators. The band consisted mainly of triangle players and drummer boys, and hit a bare minimum of right notes. In place of the Olympian gymnasts was a large pantomime lion (skin from Sachs Fifth Avenue)—the symbol of Columbia University—who bumbled blindly around for a few quaint moments. It was all very much like a rugger game between Eton and Winchester. But otherwise it is the ambition of every All-American boy to be an All-American footballer.

Nethertheless it would be unfair to paint a portrait of the American student as a complete philistine. The arts, drama, journalism, even broadcasting (for some campus compères run their own radio programmes) receive their meed of attention.

When we consider how recently it was that OUDS acquired a theatre of its own, and how frequently we found American colleges endowed not only with actual theatres for performances but even in some cases with subsidiary ones for rehearsal, we are again struck by the wealth that is everywhere so visible on the campus. Some shows that

174

we saw were superb—witness our visit to *Raisin in the Sun* at Hampton, Virginia; Some were less good—witness our visit to the opening scene of *Once Upon a Mattress* in Hiram, Ohio. But what we looked forward to with greatest anticipation—for was it not the four hundredth anniversary of the birth of the greatest English man of letters ?—was a special performance of *Romeo and Juliet* at La Salle, Philadelphia. It was perhaps the only time that Juliet has been played by an actress who stood six foot four in her socks. Sensitive to this fact the producers had procured a Romeo who stood about six foot ten. Unfortunately, to compensate, he was totally devoid of physical charm and would not have aroused a flicker of sexual emotion in the bosom of an inflamed nymphomaniac. When the play arrived at the balcony scene, instead of having to perform the usual feat of gymnastic climbing, Romeo actually *descended* on to the balcony with leggy awkwardness. At this point a student turned to his date in the row behind and said, "Now, honey, this is where the hot stuff starts". Nurse had a whine like an automatic drill from Alabama and the senior Montagu and Capulet had evidently divided between themselves a costume purloined from a local Santa Claus. The only redeeming performance was by a boy whom we were informed was a converted rock'n'roll singer and who brought a gyrating energy to the part of Mercutio. His accent was more Italianate than American; and though we were by the death scene expecting him to say "Mama mia, whatta you gotta do-a this to me-a for?" rather than "A plague on both your houses," at least we saw some correlation between actor's performance and author's intent.

Campus journalists we encountered in their hordes. On

the larger campuses indeed daily newspapers are produced, so we were able to see not only our welcome "Oxford Wits Arrive" (one of those half-true statements) but even our dismissal "Oxford Visitors depart". The genius of campus journalism (which struck us all in all as very like its Oxford couterpart) lies in the misquotation and misspelling. The traditional quip, "He is well known as a speaker for two qualities, his memory and his imagination; his memory for old jokes, and his imagination for brand-new facts" became even in the lordly Columbia year book "His memory for new jokes and old facts". The journalists themselves were different in character from the hard-bitten Oxford "pros", fresh from making a quick fiver by selling a tale of drug taking among homosexual CND abortionists to some gullible Fleet Street gossip column. One girl in Michigan who hoped to major in journalism was duped by Michael into genuinely believing that she was interviewing a Communist, whereupon she terminated the interview with an abrupt and frightened giggle. Next morning her article contained the immortal sentence, "Mr Martin Beloss, a member of British Labor, is a history scholar of eggcentric left-wing persuading".

Two emotions conflict when we consider in retrospect the impressions of our visit, those of jealousy and bewilderment. We envied the affluence displayed in architecture and assets on almost every campus. We were surprised by the seeming inability of all but a small proportion of the students either to appreciate to the full or to profit from their fortune. All the time we had this uneasy, unspoken, and maybe invidious and irrational feeling that British students would make so much better use of American facilities. Anyone from Oxford is aware that stone walls do not a prison make; but it took a visit to America to make us realise that ferro-concrete walls do not necessarily make a university. But are we naive in trying to allot to different causes the students and the facilities? After all, one can argue that Rome was too good for the barbarians; it is difficult to argue that it was too good for the Romans.

11

Anatomy of the American Student

MAN, ACCORDING to Aristotle, is a political animal. Had the Athenian philosopher ever met an American student he might have seen fit to revise his opinion. The academic year 1964–5 has been described as the year of the campus revolution. The Free Speech movement at Berkeley, California (and its more esoteric twin the Dirty Speech movement), the innovation of the teach-ins which sprouted up across the continent in the summer, have led commentators to talk in unequivocal language of an upsurge of university radicalism. Here in the seats of higher education, it is averred, the American left, so long a nomad on the highways of politics, has found a home, a shelter and a resting place. The battle of Saigon is being lost on the playing fields of Harvard. The orthodoxy of this view has been underwritten in *Time* Magazine, and in England voices are heard which compare with regret the apathy of this country's student with the idealism of his transatlantic counterpart. The transplantation of the teach-ins is hailed as another example whereby the New World is being called in to redress the balance of the Old. And for the outsider who has to rely for his opinions on the received word rather than on first-hand experience, an impression is being

178

party of the working classes—that is to say not only is it no proof, but it suggests that in fact the direct reverse is the case.

We never reached the golden coasts of the West. But there were muted echoes of the Free Speech movement in many places that we visited. In Ohio State University a group of young Liberals asked Michael if he could suggest any way in which the current policy, which forbade critics of the House Committee on Un-American activities to appear on campus, might be constructively attacked. At Purdue University, Indiana, our debate was the item on the termly programme that preceded a discussion on whether or not the university rules on visits from political speakers should be changed. In Michigan State University Michael was informed, by a somewhat embarrassed debates coach, that it was only because our visit was sponsored by the Public Events Committee and not by a political club that he was allowed to voice his views at all. It was thought that the heresies of Gaitskellite socialism might infect the clean thinking of the All-American boy. In Florida State University too the Dean's permission had to be secured before he could speak. No such check had apparently been in operation for a member of the John Birch Society who had come to the campus the week before. The son of Eton and Magdalen was seen as a herald of anarchy and subversion! In the large State universities of the Midwest and the South the conservatism of the legislatures, who control the funds for education, has apparently stifled any progress towards what we would regard as an obvious and unchallengeable liberty.

What was more sinister than this external censorship was that several faculty members to whom we talked created that comes tantalisingly close to being the exact opposite of the truth.

Our guess is that the teach-in will rank with the twist, the yo-yo and the elephant joke as one of those transient crazes that so often sweeps across America. Indeed its career in England should make us sceptical of any rival interpretation. The escalation of the English teach-in was clearly the result of inter-university mimicry rather than of a spontaneous outburst of moral protest. And in America itself the phenomenon was not all pervasive. The Ivy League universities and the giant education laboratories of the West Coast where it was born are about as typical of American colleges as Eton and Bedales are of English secondary schools. Even on these campuses it is hard to estimate how much the initiative came from the teachers, how much from the students. Again, although the teach-in is said to be a revelation of protest, in fact in character and form it is a method of instruction. Both sides of the case are presented. It is indeed an extended debate. And does anyone call a debate a form of protest? The reason that the teach-ins have attracted so much attention is that the notion of any form of criticism of government policy from the left, even if it is voiced in comparatively standard opinions, is remarkable for the American university. Yet they have engaged a powerful sympathy that conceals their real significance. Liberals should cheer not because teach-ins are representative, but because they are there at all. They represent a start of, not the conclusion of an argument. Their existence of a general radicalism among American students the same way as the presence of a grammar a Conservative cabinet is proof that the To endorsed the policy as correct as well as expedient. Politics had no place on a campus. Students were not responsible enough to be allowed a free hand in the organisation of their own affairs. Compared to those that exist on many campuses, proctorial rules at Oxford are a constitution of liberty. Many students to whom we spoke were genuinely surprised to learn that at Oxford the only censorship that was exercised sprang from the discretion of the under-graduates, and that Communist and Fascist alike could have a platform if not an uninterrupted hearing. Before we talk of the Free Speech movement as a significant stage in the development of the democratic process, we should remember that what the students of California and their kind are demanding is something that in England we would find it difficult to believe that they had ever been denied. And what is disturbing is not that they should demand these rights, but that there should be any opposition to their demands. As for the Dirty Speechers we should see here only evidence of the ease with which a serious cause can be damaged by the intrusion of frivolities and irrelevances. The graffiti on lavatory walls, though they may adorn the treasury of a nation's wit, have never been seen as carvings on the sacred tablets of liberty. If the battles for freedom from faculty control are won, we shall be able to celebrate one of the outstanding victories of the nineteenth century.

It is moreover far from clear that a majority of the students in the areas in which this activity is taking place have any spirit of kinship with the activists. It is after all very easy for a group of militants to win headlines. A band of one thousand may seem a powerful force; in the context of a campus of thirty thousand students it is in fact a fringe movement. This point has been repeatedly stressed by

181

American friends with whom we have since communicated. Those who are seriously concerned about the quality of student commitment should not allow themselves to be misled by journalists whose habit it is to cloak with the tidy generalisation the complex, and to inflate the insignificant with the bold superlative. Readers of the English popular press might conclude that Oxford is a community of pacifist drug addicts. There is, to say the least, evidence to support alternative view-points.

The bulk of American students remain obdurate conservatives, conservative in politics, conformist in morals, conservative in the style of their behaviour and in the range of their ambitions, conservative above all in that they show little eagerness to form any distinct philosophy, be it reactionary or progressive, on these matters. This is of course our personal view-point. It may be argued that in our travels around the campuses, by some coincidence, we met only that small fraction of the residents who would deserve the epithets with which we have chosen to grace them. We readily admit that we too are making our own generalisations. Maybe hidden in fraternity houses that we never entered, lurking in classes we never attended, collecting in arenas we never crossed, there gathered that great mass of radical, questioning, above all representative American youth of whom we have since with such astonishment read so much. If that is the case we freely apologise. But we would guess that those who acted as our hosts, and those who went out of their way to meet and talk to us, were in fact the more articulate section of the campus. And though many of them did not in any way conform to the description that we have given, they would and did agree with it. We record not just what Oxford students

182

thought of American students, but what American students thought of themselves.

Politics plays a role in quadrangle that it never would on campus. It is a possibly regrettable, but easily observable, fact that in Oxford the coveted positions in the student hierarchy are contested on a basis of rival political affiliation. Indeed the techniques of politics are also borrowed. There is a whiff of Tammany Hall in the precincts of the Oxford Union; and amateur psephologists, hot from Nuffield tutorials, can detect in recent battles for the Presidency the operation of the swing of the pendulum. The infection has even spread to the elections to the Presidency of the Junior Common Rooms, where a miniature class war is fought out between the public school Conservatives and the grammar school Socialists. In an American university political beliefs are considered to be as private as moral practice is over here. Certainly no one to whom we talked thought that the heads of public forums, the presidents of fraternities, the campus Pooh-Bahs, could be appointed or elected on such an irrelevant criterion. Fitness for the job plus photogenic quality were the foremost considerations. Moreover the politicos themselves, the leaders of the Young Republicans or the Young Democrats had no special status on the campus. In Oxford the President of a political club has by contrast a definite cachet beyond that attributed to the leading folk dancer or the captain of the water polo team.

If political views are discounted as subsidiary in the daily life of the student, political careers are rarely the ambition of the most gifted young men and women on campus. In Oxford of course at any Christ Church cocktail party the rooms will be full of self-appointed future Prime

183

Ministers, and every prominent undergraduate believes that he carries a scrambler telephone in his attaché case. Even what Lord David Cecil has described as the lesser bicycling colleges contain more embryo MPs and civil servants than is found in the whole Midwest. Those who have no special talent or impelling vocation are apt to think of politics as an ultimate, if not an immediate, goal. But in America we could have counted those who sought careers in public service in single figures. There are a multitude of reasons for this that were frequently offered by way of explanation to us. Money was clearly an important factor. It was a trifle odd that so many of those who stoutly contested the proposition that "From Log Cabin to White House is No Longer Possible in America today" with a wealth of evidence, culled, alas, from the age of Lincoln, should themselves be living examples of its truth. The House of Commons may still be an expensive club for those without independent means, but there is at least no "entrance fee". In America all the evidence foretells the capture of Congress by a small political plutocracy. Flimsy legislative checks on campaign expenditure; the opportunities suggested by the mass media for publicity and propaganda; the examples of mechanised politics offered by Kennedy's capture of the Presidency and Goldwater's smash-and-grab raid on the Republican nomination in 1960; all these constituted a threat to the democratic process, and suggested that the leaders of tomorrow's America will either be the rich or the pawns of the rich. Many were prepared to concede in private what they had denied on the platform.

The bright young man cannot simply decide that he wishes to enter politics and then seek adoption by some

184

constituency party. The carpet-bagger, as the fate of Pierre Salinger in the California Senatorial race revealed, is a little-loved figure on the American political scene. Accident of birth or residence may dictate to the ambitious young man where his political career is to start, and "Who wants to be a big shot in North Dakota?" as one prominent and politics-conscious Ivy League debater told us. Within these limits that convention has imposed the party machine holds sway. For those liberals that we met in the South the problem was especially acute. There just didn't seem to be a way to break in. Who would appoint, who would publish, who would even listen? For the most gifted, fresh from the Arcadias of the big law schools, there was admittedly the prospect of a niche on Capitol Hill, employment in the office of some senator with the prospects of further advancement, but for the small-time college boy there would be travel on the footpaths, not the highways. A friend of ours from La Salle College, Philadelphia, described his own plans. "First, I'll put in some census work at the local party Headquarters . . . then maybe in a couple of years they might make me delegate to a Convention . . . then perhaps I could get in on the Governor's staff. . . ." It all seemed very uncertain to us. The only other real enthusiast we encountered, in Denison, Ohio, had a far more carefree attitude. "Oh sure, I want to be a pol. But I don't reckon on choosing my party awhile yet."

It is of course clear that our impressions of this side of student interest were bound to be biased. There is nothing in America that corresponds to the Oxford–Cambridge axis, no place, attendance at which confers an automatic stamp of "difference", a passport to destiny. This was refreshing and healthy—and explained to a certain extent this curious lack of interest in public life which may not truly have been lacking, but simply dissipated among select individuals or different campuses. To a certain extent, but not wholly. The one emotion that struck us as disheartening and pervasive was in fact a disdain for politics as represented by the politicians. Paradoxically, if we had to select the one theme that recurred most often in our conversations from place to place (discounting questions about our impressions of America as being matters of courtesy, and questions about the Beatles as being matters of religion), it was the impact of the late President Kennedy. There can hardly have been a campus which we visited where at some moment some person would not ask us what our reactions had been when we heard the news of the assassination. In some unique way people's memory of that moment had become frozen and undiminished. They would describe with great accuracy the shock, the disbelief, the tears—who had told them, where they had been, what they had to leave unfinished. "Hardly anyone went out of doors for two whole days," someone said. "They just stayed inside and watched and waited." And when the anniversary came round—we were in Illinois at the time—it was treated almost as a secular Christmas, but one whose meaning was still remembered. Even in this, however, there was a fringe of cynicism, and some asked us why it was that Kennedy had made so much of a mark in Europe, so much more of a mark, that is, than he had made in his own country.

But grudging or ungrudging, the foremost note was that of respect; and it's clear that the reactions to the current generation of political leaders are coloured by the contrast. The comparison that was everywhere made between the high standard of the Kennedy–Nixon contest and the

186

gutter brawl of the 1964 campaign was very noticeable. Both Kennedy in America in 1960 and Wilson in Britain in 1964 won their victories by extremely narrow margins. It is fair to compare them if not as political figures at least as bearers of a new political message which seemed particularly to be aimed at the young. Both followed on after administrations which, whatever their virtues, had seemed cosy, conservative, unchallenging. However far the growing disillusion with the Labour government may spread, it was at least seen at the time of the election by a significant proportion of British students as something that might solve the frustrations of nearly a decade of protest and self-question. Kennedy had maybe a more difficult task. He had first to create an awareness that all was not perfect in God's own country. Once the spark was struck, his support burgeoned. Yet for all the brave words at the time, it would appear to us that the impetus of the New Frontier ground to a halt on campus with the death of its leader. Young Americans prefer rather to follow a man, than to realise a vision. All the pragmatic talk of Johnson failed to evoke anything but a nostalgia for his predecessor. The fact that the problems that the Texan emphasised, those of poverty, of race relations, of education, were closer to their own immediate lives than the more fine-spun world-view of Kennedy made no impression. Students seemed sickened by the whole business of the 1964 election. "A fool against a knave", that was the predominant attitude. There seemed to be no more love for the Great society of the Democrats than for the Out-of-Date society of the Republicans. So we too found little evidence that the "intellectualism" of Kennedy had stimulated a response on the campuses. The basic tone of American political life is folksy, not cerebral.

187

There is a long tradition of anti-intellectualism that claims Adlai Stevenson as its most recent victim. In Britian it takes a Lord Salisbury to excavate that kind of sentiment. But it does not seem that his neolithic opinions have had noticeable effect on the British political scene. "Too clever by half" he called Iain Macleod. There are men leading Britain today, whom he calls "Too clever by three-quarters" if his knowledge of compound fractions extended that far. And Britain has never had an aggressively anti-intellectual leader like Andrew Jackson; or for that matter Lyndon Johnson. In America there is still no belief that a university, or at any rate a university education, is necessary for a political career, and still the residue of a view that it is a positive handicap. There is therefore no implicit reason why the student should tend to politics just because he has been a student.

Most important of all in any analysis of why politics fails to fascinate or to stimulate the ambition of young Americans is an emphasis on the basically anti-political nature of American ideology. Since Balfour's original dictum it has often been argued in this country that whichever party is in power, the Tories by the medium of the establishment are in control. But in fact in Britain today, whichever party is elected to office, the Labour party's philosophy dominates. That is to say, we have come to accept that government can and indeed should solve all our problems. Anyone who contests this as a ludicrous generalisation should study the language of the popular press, which is after all both the vehicle for and the promoter of our national ideology at its lowest level. Everything from the outbreak of typhoid in a northern city to the break-out of a train robber in a southern one is blamed directly or indirectly on the Government. Quite naturally in such an atmosphere the person who seeks power and influence turns to politics as the career which leads one to the centre of the stage. But in America a different vision holds sway. The grip of the old laissez-faire notions has slackened but slightly. That government is best which governs, if not least, at any rate as little as is decently possible. Therefore if it is grudgingly acknowledged that politicians are pre-eminent in the attention that they attract, there is an inborn prejudice against their meddling and interference. The independent young man would rather be an anti-politician.

The echoes of the presidential campaign reverberated around the campuses. Mock elections seemed to be held everywhere. Johnson seemed to win in most places, except in the Southern and the extreme low church colleges. Goldwater usually ran second, though he had the odd challenge from the ubiquitous Ringo Starr, Norman Thomas, Micky Mantle and Strom Thurmond. Campus newsboards were decked out in the literature of political warfare; quotations from Goldwater threatening to send ICBMs into the Kremlin lavatories, or juxtaposed inconsistencies gleaned from Johnson's volatile career. There were many badges worn, many stickers on the student Chevrolets, many signs of an external partisanship not matched by any innate commitment. It reminded one a little of Montagus and Capulets—an artificial contest, a glorified slanging match. Personality was all-important, issue mattered very little.

Many of the reasons why students are unpolitical in interest are similar to those why they are unpolitical as regards careers. But one might add others, some purely

189

technical. In English universities interest is fostered by political clubs who arrange for visits from distinguished speakers. As England is a small country, in which there are few universities, such speakers can be obtained with varying degrees of ease. On an American campus the chances of an address by a single senator per semester are, as we discovered, small. This creates a gulf between students and politicians which does not exist in England to anything like the same extent. Secondly, there is the faculty policy which in so many places is, as we have illustrated, hostile to the whole idea of political controversy on the campus. It is worth speculating why it is that in America, where scholastic syllabuses are normally so closely linked to the activities of everyday life, this reactionary attitude should be taken. No one on the faculty objects to the production of embryo journalists, business men, or even professional football stars. Thirdly, there are the constrictions of the method of debate. Debates are after all a useful way of clarifying political issue and engendering political belief. In America where debates are treated as an academic exercise, and all the emphasis is placed on how one marshalls a case and not on what case one marshalls, this advantage is forfeited. In Wabash College, Indiana, the debates coach had refused to let his team enter for any further tournaments since he was deeply disturbed by the apathy that the system produced towards the deeper issues of politics. Finally, there is the ever pernicious influence of the fraternities in which political interest would be considered as a sign of bad taste, and the general air is one of unthinking "correct" Republicanism. We remember in Madison how one of our hosts, an articulate and engaging person, claimed quite seriously that the Young Democrats on campus took part in political discussions and so on because they were the flotsam and jetsam of the campus population who were not really acceptable in any decent circle. He himself was Chairman of the Young Republicans, but it did not seem that his post involved any political activity at all. Quite typically he made in the evening a witty, radical speech in favour of the Welfare State.

No one would deny that such movements as SNIC are student run and student filled, nor that students have responded to the call for practical help in the War on Poverty. But the fact that students may head these activities does not mean that students as a class are activists.

One of the first things that we discovered in talking with Americans about America is that they had strong reservations about whether we should be talking about the subject at all. Our original list of debates had contained some motions of a European slant, some of a contemporary American one, and some common to both categories. A subtle censorship by the Institute of International Education excised anything that smacked of controversy. All our motions that implied criticism of Goldwater, for example "That a Why Not Victory? foreign policy can only lead to defeat", were removed from the list. Presumably considerations other than those of maintaining the special relationship weighed against "That Sexual Intercourse Is only Justified in the Marriage Bed". While we somewhat resented the interference with our choice of preferences, it is to be noted that the palm for folly must go to the British Foreign Office for their attitude towards an Oxford team in Germany in 1965. In the interests of international cordiality they were not allowed to *propose* the motion that "This House Deplores American Leadership in Europe". They

191

were instead allowed to *oppose* the motion "That this House Welcomes American Leadership in Europe".

At all events we were left with at least three motions that were specifically American in theme: "That the Power of the American Judiciary is too Great", "That from Log Cabin to White House is No Longer Possible in America Today", and "That America Has Failed to Advance to the New Frontier". Whenever we were to debate one of these someone was sure to come up to us before the debate (and sometimes, alas, after it) and say that as English we had no right to discuss such matters. It was a very smart lady at Columbia who set this particular conversational ball rolling. As she revealed herself as a wife of the judge, on that occasion apprehension was added to our irritation. At St Joseph's College, Philadelphia, a drunken Jesuit claimed more broadly that no Englishman could ever hope to understand America. "Not even Denis Brogan?" "No, not even Denish Brogan!" This idea that there was something about America that made it understandable exclusively by native Americans was ludicrous, especially when one considers firstly how diverse a country America is, and secondly of what various origins the Americans themselves are. We wondered how well acquainted our Irish priest was with the attitudes of a Mississippi Negro or a Brooklyn Jew. Anyhow, what do they know of America, who only America know? We cannot believe that strangers in English universities would ever be made to feel that they were discussing topics on sufferance. Indeed our experience in the Oxford Union is that people take a positive pleasure in hearing their country not only discussed, but criticized. We resented this recurrent attitude not least because, as we explained on frequent occasions, what concerns America

192

concerns Britain, however untrue the reverse may be in these post-Imperial days. Nor would the Americans allow us to poke gentle fun at their leaders. In England a healthy bi-partisanship exists as far as wit is concerned. A Socialist will applaud a well-turned cut at Harold Wilson as long as it is really amusing, and same tolerance is true of the Tories. But if we let slip some crack about Barry Goldwater the whole of one side of the audience would erupt with boos and catcalls. Michael invariably hung out a red rag for them. "Using the Bible as a textbook of economics (titters), Barry Goldwater (boos and cheers), that great ex-future President of the USA (louder boos), came to the conclusion in *Conscience of a Conservative* in which he expressed his desire to take the American people on his great march forward into the past (howls and catcalls)— this came just before the chapter in which he advocated the repeal of the Declaration of Independence (cries of "Go home to Peking") *he* came to the conclusion that the poor could help themselves. I myself have always thought that Goldwater's economic ideas owe more to Adam than to Adam Smith (pandemonium)"—and so on. After a few sessions like this the 1964 Republican convention brawls became quite credible.

Americans moreover cannot bear to have their institutions as such criticised, although of course they are prepared to criticise the men who run them. In a debate in the Merchant Marine Academy, Long Island, we were made to feel quite embarrassed by an opponent who in an excess of patriotic zeal shouted out, "These Englishmen are attacking the Supreme Court. Therefore they are attacking our Constitution. Therefore they are attacking the will of the people." This was only an extreme case of what frequently occurred. There was a mystical belief in the virtues of the American Constitution, and there were few who were prepared to concede that a constitution, conceived in the circumstance of the eighteenth century, might not function to perfection in the twentieth. We cannot believe that there would be the same emotional commitment in Britain to some part of the machinery of government. Even if people (and then not university students!) are apt to resent attacks on the Queen, this does not mean that there is the same intolerance to discussions about the merits and demerits of the monarchy. In our debates on the Supreme Court we were apt to get the impression, as we praised the British system of government in contrast to the American separation of powers, that our audience resented us because they felt that we were calling on them to swear once more allegiance to the Crown. A sophisticated form of neo-colonialism! And yet it is the British people who are supposed to be complacent with regard to their institutions.

Similarly it is British people who are supposed to find the be-all-and-end-all rebuttal in the phrase "It's the British way of doing things, and it must work for us". Yet how often did we hear Americans justify some practice by saying that "It's the American way". Michael remembers an extraordinary conversation in Ohio on the eve of a debate on the Welfare State with a young American girl who was full of praise for the British people and full of fear for British ideas. She recited a garbled account of what she called "The American capitalist tradition", and treated the Constitution with the same reverence as if it were the Ten Commandments. This once again was not a unique occurrence. And what we are trying to stress is not what it was that was said, not what the merits or demerits were of

194

the "philosophies" expounded to us, but the methods of approach to issues. There is, at the best, the same residue of prejudice, of unquestioned belief, of underlying assumption in the American mind as there is in the British, though it takes different forms. Indeed, if one had to chose, one would say that it is the young American who is by far the less sceptical and irreverent towards the "received truths".

The most potent myth that infects the young American is the myth of the Opportunity State. It gradually became apparent to us that the vision of the New Frontier could have little meaning to those who were still seeking for the old frontier. The Log Cabin motion and the discussions that it provoked emphasised to what extent young Americans still believed that theirs was a society of almost limitless possiblity. There was a hangover from the "Go West Young Man" days of a century earlier. Then the frontier beckoned to the ambitious and there were prospects of new riches to be sought beyond the horizon. This (and the view is historical orthodoxy) naturally created an attitude of individualism, but above all of hope. But the faith that America is somehow unique has persisted into an age when the last frontier has been reached, when it is swelling suburbs and not distant prairies that cater for the growing population, where the problems that face America are those that face the majority of Western industrial democratic societies. Somewhat naturally this continuing faith inhibits a rational and empirical approach to political and social problems. Some of the people who voiced these sentiments, it is true, were themselves the children of immigrants; and their mentality was one that characterises the successful immigrant, the tendency to eulogise the country in which he has settled at the expense

195

of that from which he came. But to say that this explains the dominant ideology is simply to pretend that the pattern of the nineteenth century is repeating itself; rather one might seek the clue in the expansion of a system of higher education.

The educational merits and demerits of the universalisation of the university has been discussed in an earlier chapter. But we would like to throw out what may be simply a wild speculation as to the social effects of the system. It is widely believed that almost all American teenagers reach the university. This is, of course, untrue. But, as we have shown, the proportion, which varies from State to State (it reaches as high as fifty per cent in California) and which is rapidly expanding, is far higher than in Britain. This means that if one were to apply the phrase "Two Nations" to America, one would have to draw the line not between a tiny élite and a large majority as in Britain, but between, say, one-third and two-thirds of the population. For those who graduate from university, the world may indeed seem their oyster. But for those who do not it may appear somewhat differently. It was after all the democratic nature of their educational system that was used most frequently to illustrate to us why the "American dream" is no idle reverie. If we seek analogy with the British experience, we might find it in the gulf between the grammar school boy and the boy from the secondary mod. It would be ridiculous to cavil at a society like America which can offer higher education to such a significant proportion of its youth. But we might deduce from what has happened there that all societies must have élites, that equality is a mirage sought by idealists. At least we must recognise that a meritocracy is not very tolerant of those who fail to attain

196

the standards which it sets; and there is a problem common to America and to Britian, even though in America the division between success and reject is made at seventeen plus. For, whatever may be the American mistrust of intellectuals in politics, the college degree is the new key to the doors of the Affluent Society. The get-rich-quick days are over, and the sagas of future moguls of industry will be of the drip-dry-to-riches variety. What the American students who eulogise their system fail to appreciate is its effect on those who are excluded from its benefits. Why they fail to appreciate it is because they are included in them.

Americans are very fond of saying that there is really no difference between their two parties. That is to say they are implicitly denying that there is any of the albeit muted class war that erupts at General Election time in Britain. But this impression that they try to convey is totally at odds with the impression that is in fact given. All the foreign students to whom we spoke agreed that the American on campus is a predominantly Republican animal. Campus liberals too bemoaned a certain type of college boy Republican as a betrayer of his background in just the same way as left wingers in English universities level their mockery at the Conservative grammar school boy who is thought to be climbing on to the Establishment band-wagon. It is beyond the walls of the campus that the Democrat strength lies in the Jerichos of urban America.

The Welfare State motion served best as a litmus paper of student opinion. We divided on this issue: Jonathan taking an Enoch Powell approach and Michael an orthodox Labour line. The allies whom we were given were, alas, of very different stripe. Jonathan would usually be em-

197

barrased by a Goldwaterite of radical views, who would inveigh against Franklin Roosevelt and old age pensions. Michael would be supported (hardly a mot juste) by a middle-of-the-road Democrat, who would agree with every word that Jonathan said, and would regard Michael as a kind of extremist heretic who ought to be deported at the very least. Since the turn of the century in Britain the need for the State to aid the old and the indigent has been recognised by the provision of ever-increasing assistance; and today one cannot think of a politician who would denounce the idea. Indeed the apparatus of the Beveridge Welfare State with its blanket benefits is accepted by all but a few; and moderate though Jonathan's argument—that those who could afford to do so should pay for their welfare services—was, the idea is as yet too sophisticated for most English political platforms. For the young Americans, however, he touched the limits of permissible leftism. Michael was quite beyond the pale. Whenever he extolled the virtues of State benefits as the right of every citizen in an affluent society, he provoked menacing rumbles, punctuated by cries of "Redski" and "Pinko" from the audience. His American colleague, scarcely knowing which way to look, would usually argue in favour of the War on Poverty and the Medicare Bill, leaving Jonathan's partner to conclude by saying that there could be no need for a Welfare State in America since she already had one and had had one since the days of the New Deal. How unexpected were the kind of arguments that Michael put forward can be shown by the fact that in Akron, Ohio, whereas thirty per cent of the audience had said that they were in favour of his proposition before the debate began, only five per cent adherence remained at the end of his speech. Was Jonathan's eloquence alone responsible for this swing? Even he had doubts.

Clearly for the majority of the audience the real debate on this issue had not begun when we sat down. Irritated rightists used to surround Jonathan afterwards over coffee and cookies and demand why he had left their case undefended. "That damn Commie Jew friend of yours ought to be lynched," said one of them, evidently mistaking Michael for Trotsky. "Why's Douglas-Home gonna put up old age pensions?" asked another plaintively. "Is this some kinda sell-out?" That basis of common assumption about the duties owed by the State to its citizens, and by those citizens to each other, which would be present in a debate on such a topic in England was totally lacking in America. Only once was Michael given a fellow speaker who agreed with his point of view. Only once did he win the motion, and then at Madison where the audience was comprised mainly of foreigners, and of Brooklyn Jews, who had come this far to seek a college education because of the quota system that operated in universities in their native State. And then the local newspaper, an organ of prairie conservatism, somewhat diminished the triumph by coldly reporting: "Beloff's main argument was that in a Welfare State unemployment benefits would not be given to those who were employed".

The kind of questions that would be asked from the floor showed how large the gulf was that separated us from the majority of the young Americans. "Why does my neighbour's poverty give him the right to my wealth?" asked one. Another argued that "The people who live in the Chicago slums live there because that's where they like to live." Constantly the theme was reiterated: "If you give

199

people something for nothing, you'll take away their initiative to work. If you give elderly free medical aid, you'll make them wards of the Federal Government." How Michael came to love the sound of a friendly English, Indian or African accent in rare support from the floor. At one place in Florida a local doctor came up in high dudgeon afterwards, and asked why we had been given visas if we'd just come to laugh at the free enterprise system that had made America what it was today. There was nothing that the Americans liked better than to hear that Harold Macmillan received an old age pension, or that under the National Health Service there was so little hospital space that maternity beds had to be booked up ten months in advance. The popularity that Johnson enjoyed as President was, as far as we could see, not the result of any true respect for his social policies but stemmed from the fear that many had thought that Goldwater was the angel of death come down to earth.

For all their expertise with the ready statistic, we found that on the whole the debaters whom we encountered were unable to evaluate the American condition in terms of the experience of other countries. For example, despite a mass of evidence to prove it they rarely seemed able to understand that the level of unemployment in America was higher than that in any European country of equivalent kind. It was apparently inconceivable to them that this could be so. Nor often would they believe statistics about the extent of sickness and poverty in their own country. Many of them thought that this was some kind of fictitious debating point. In England too, of course, the sudden revelations of American poverty have come as something of a surprise after a decade in which all we have read

200

about have been the problems of excessive affluence, of surplus, and of planned obsolescence. But at least we are not inhibited in believing in the new picture by thoughts that we are somehow unpatriotic in so doing.

This attitude all stems from the fanatical individualism that underlies their whole philosophy. After one debate in Ohio a young Virginian approached Michael and said that whether Virginia was a poor State or not, she didn't want any federal aid. Virginia could solve her own problems. Michael suggested that perhaps he himself hadn't really experienced poverty, that it was maybe a little presumptuous of him to set himself up as a vox pauperum. But he was made to feel a little ashamed in so doing. The boy was the son of a miner. He was paying his own way through college. His job as a kind of clerk took him thirty hours a week; his studies somewhere near forty. He was married with a small daughter. "Sometimes I don't see her for two days or so." No one could argue that he was some rich young man, careless and ignorant of the problems of the workers. No doubt he felt that his own energy and initiative entitled him to scorn those who lacked those qualities. It was at least a credible, if not necessarily a justifiable, attitude. There is something of the old Puritan in the philosophy: an emphasis on the value of independence and self-reliance. In some ways the best book to read on the contemporary American mind remains Tawney's *Religion and the Rise of Capitalism*.

That Michael's milk-and-water socialism was something of a revelation was shown by more than the spontaneous audience reaction. The campus newspapers had little time for unbiased reporting. They would go so far as to praise a "brave effort" (Ohio) or speak of audiences "perhaps already convinced the other way" (Illinois). But after the debate he would be approached by a small claque of campus liberals who would express in an embarrassingly effusive manner their delight that someone should actually be allowed on campus to say the kind of things that he had said. Michael, who at Oxford is regarded as something of a Tory in Socialist's clothing (a somewhat inaccurate view since his favourite dress is a pinstripe with an Old Etonian tie), was now regarded as a messiah of radicalism. The ghetto mentality of the campus leftists was both fascinating and alarming. In Wilkes Barre, Pennsylvania, in the heart of Appalachia, the debates coach, a man of engaging radical persuasion (he would turn to us every so often and say, "Why doesn't your Queen give away her jewels to the poor?"), was vehement on the subject of how the image of Britain's Welfare State was distorted in the American press. "Lies, lies, lies!" he shouted, as he took Michael on a tour of the barren, wasted mining countryside. And generally by the end of the evening, spent in sentimental conversations about placard, poster, picket and all the other paraphernalia of protest, there would be emotional good wishes and almost tearful farewells exchanged. And Michael would take his leave, feeling like some messenger who had come to a beleaguered garrison bearing tidings of hope from the great world outside.

It was the rarity with which we encountered people of viewpoints analogous to our own which made them seem so very attractive to us. Anyone who has endured three years or more in the Oxford monde politique swiftly tires of the stale Marxist rhetoric of those who have never read a a word of Marx, and the urgent sense of brotherhood with the working classes of those who have never done a day's

work in their lives, of chip-on-the-shoulder radicals whose
so-called socialism was the result of personal inadequacies.
Those American liberals whom we met were genuinely
sympathetic, intelligent and industrious, and all the more
impressive because they were so few in number. No angry
young American dramatist could ever write "There are no
good, brave causes left". It was, it seemed to us, all too
easy in America to see which were the forces of progress
and which of reaction. The struggle for equal opportunity
for the Negro, the war on poverty, the battle for Medicare,
all these would easily enlist our sympathy. In England, on
the other hand, in all but the field of sexual morals,
the great victories of the liberal ideal have been won, and
the controversies between the parties are exaggerated in an
artificial manner. But whereas in England the student
politicos are inevitably to the left of their parties (How
many university Tories believe in an independent deterrent,
capital punishment or the public schools? How many
university Socialists believe in the American alliance, an
incomes policy, or check on immigration?), in America the
government is, in domestic affairs at least, far in advance of
the great bulk of campus opinion. "Why American students," writes Irving Kristol in the August edition of
Encounter, "amidst general prosperity and under a liberal
administration that is expanding the Welfare State more
aggressively and successfully than anyone had thought
possible, should 'go left', is a riddle to which no sociologist
has as yet come up with an answer." One answer might be
that this movement to the left is a figment of the imagination of journalists shaken by a spasm of wishful thinking.
There is just no riddle for the sociologist to solve. As for
Mr Isaac Deutscher who has spoken of the rebirth of

American Marxism, on the strength of a visit to Harvard, one can only conclude that he is an inverted Senator McCarthy.

We met one young couple who had volunteered for the Peace Corps, and only a handful who had participated in any kind of Civil Rights demonstration. Nor was it apparent that there was a new sentiment of radicalism in foreign affairs. Can it be, we innocently enquire, that the indignation over Vietnam stems from the fact that the Americans are losing the fight there and that American lives are being squandered? When was there a teach-in over the Dominican invasion? Was there a teach-in over Cuba three years back? We would suggest that what is being assaulted is what Denis Brogan has called "the illusion of American omnipotence". Whenever we debated the United Nations we would meet people who were suspicious of anything that might seem to thwart the American anti-Communist crusade. What was sought was less peace than the Pax Americana. There is little trace of the old isolationism. Indeed when we were questioned about foreign policy, what was always to the forefront was a feeling that Britain might somehow be betraying America by pulling the punches of her support. Those buses to Cuba have left their tyre marks on the American mind. In Edinboro State, Pennsylvania, a caucus of faculty members berated Britain for fence sitting and equivocations. It took our sharp reminder about the burden Britain bore in two World Wars while America washed her hands the while to make them feel that the grievances were not all on one side.

No, it is not unrest about the imperialist tide of American foreign policy that we remember on the campus in 1964! What impressed us most was that there was a sizeable group who espoused the cause of Senator Goldwater. We defy any commentator to assert that this particular faction does not outnumber by far any band of dissidents over Vietnam. We remember one encounter in Eastern Nazarone College, Boston, with particular clarity. We were struck by the blazing faith of these disciples. After we had said we would like to have an informal discussion with the local Goldwater supporters, an emaciated, myopic, lank-haired, acne-pitted Goliath was summoned to make a frenzied statement of the creed. He spoke at machine-gun pace, occasionally running his hands through his hair, and saying in a frenzied voice "Oh hell, I've forgotten the arguments". On the home front there were anti-government action "which is Socialism which is Communism" (an oft-repeated political equation). But abroad—ah, there was the rub! These young Americans regretted that the Administration hadn't dropped the atom bomb on Korea, supported the Bay of Pigs with aircraft, suspended all foreign aid to neutral countries, and launched all-out war on Vietnam. Every now and again they would all chorus in rhythm, "Berlin, Cuba, Laos", and thump the table as if they were driving nails into the coffin of the American way of life.

Essentially the Goldwater movement was an anti-political one. The closest analogy in recent British politics would be CND. It was the basis of the Goldwater case that their jet boy hero had not compromised himself in any way. "He votes for what he believes in; not because it gets him support." By contrast Johnson was a wheeler-dealer, an equivocator, a trimmer. They never grasped, as CND supporters have never grasped, that it's not enough to be righteous; one must also be effective. If we pointed out to

205

them that Goldwater would do a little better if he moved towards the centre plateau of political belief rather than patrolling the frontiers as the lone ranger of the right, they thought that we were asking him to commit an unpardonable sin. They would rather curse the darkness than light a candle. It is a paradox that these young people, whose vision of the world was so different from that of the Aldermaston marchers, should share their naïvety, their blinkered viewpoint, and be inspired by the same frustrations about the complexity of the situation with which they were confronted.

We were never conscious of any feeling of youthful rebellion on the campus. In England people will shake their heads over student antics and chorus, "Well, they'll grow out of it". In America there is no need for such self-given consolations. The student is already prematurely middle-aged. He wishes not to change the world, but to fit into it. There is no sign of any novelty in style: no Beatle-type hair cuts, no fancy gear, mainly the college-crested sweatshirt for the sun, and sober jacket for the cold. They were all well-scrubbed, well-mannered, well-fed, well-intentioned and the same. Peter Seeger in his "Little Boxes" number has trapped American society in a song. The complacency is claustrophobic. There may be some who sow their wild oats, but if there are they produce a poor enough harvest. They are more likely to ape the attitudes of their parents than to question them. And they admit this quite freely. "I don't know why we're so conservative," sighed a Florida State sophomore, "I guess that when we ask questions in class we get conservative answers." Too glib, too unsubtle? "You've got to remember," said a Jesuit scholar at La Salle, "these college boys and girls are just echoing what they've always heard. Most of them don't know what poverty's about. They live in big city suburbs, far away from the poor and the Negroes. Few of them have any idea about war or what it's like. They don't even remember Korea. For eight years they were taught that everything was going fine. You can't blame them in not looking for trouble, or for failing to understand that what they've been told wasn't the whole truth. And don't you think that maybe when you talk of the radical, critical character of English students you're only talking about a minority? And how many of that minority are sincere; and how many just playing a part? What will happen when they too look for jobs, a wife, want to have a house and children?" Sound common sense or Jesuitry?

On almost our last day in America we lunched with a high official in the British Information Service in New York, and gave him our impression. "You know," he said, "you mustn't be too harsh. People often say that all the talk about the difference between us because the Americans only have two hundred years of independent history, and we British have had a thousand, is just nonsense. But it isn't. They genuinely feel the British have got some sort of inheritance that they lack. They hate criticism because they're still unsure of themselves. And yet, it's just that uncertainty that prompts them always to ask how you find them, do you like them. They turn a blind eye to much of the violence and squalor and tension that exists around them, because most of them are cradled by prosperity. They cling to their own traditions because this gives them a feeling of continuity; they like their rituals because it creates a pattern.

"But remember all the energy, the curiosity, all the go

207

you've found here. It isn't all turned to selfish ends. And remember what you don't like about England: the slowness, the stuffiness, the particular brand of insularity. We two countries have got a lot to learn from each other still. But as you've discovered, it isn't all a case of the Old World having to learn from the New."

Jonathan Aitken & Michael Beloff

JONATHAN AITKEN and MICHAEL BELOFF have several things in common. Both are Oxford University graduates, both served as president of the Oxford Union, and in the summer of 1964 both were chosen to represent Oxford in a debating tour of America. Both are from distinguished families—Mr. Aitken is a grandson of Lord Beaverbrook and Mr. Beloff is a son of Max Beloff. Both are intensely interested in politics; however, Mr. Beloff is a Socialist and Mr. Aitken a Conservative.